D0532785

The Princes Gate Collection

Courtauld Institute Galleries, Woburn Square, London WC1H 0AA

*This exhibition and catalogue
have been sponsored by
National Westminster Bank*

At NatWest we feel it right to assist through our community support
programme a wide range of activities which contribute towards the
quality of life in the society of which we are a part.

We support projects in a social field, in sport and in both the performing
and visual arts. We are, therefore, delighted to be able to sponsor the
first public viewing of this highly important and hitherto private
collection.

Robin Leigh-Pemberton
Chairman
National Westminster Bank

Cover: Sir Peter Paul Rubens
The Family of Jan Brueghel the Elder (detail) cat.66

ISBN 0 904563 04 9

Published by the Trustees of the Home House Society
for the Courtauld Institute of Art
University of London 1981

Designed by Graham Johnson/Lund Humphries
Printed by Lund Humphries, London & Bradford

Contents

Foreword

When this exhibition opens to the public on 17 July at the Courtauld Institute Galleries it will be the first time that the Princes Gate Collection, formed by Count Antoine Seilern, has been exhibited in a public gallery. Individual paintings and drawings were lent to exhibitions by Count Seilern in his lifetime, and the collection was always made accessible to scholars and students. We hope and believe that visitors to the exhibition will be thrilled by the range and quality of the paintings and drawings on show, and that they will derive great pleasure and inspiration from them. For Count Seilern wished others to share the life-enhancing experience that he himself derived from the study of great master-pieces.

The Collection has been bequeathed to the Home House Society Trustees, the Trust that was set up in 1931 by Samuel Courtauld when he endowed the Courtauld Institute of Art and gave to the University of London the magnificent foundation collection which bears his name. The Courtauld Institute of Art, in particular, and the University of London of which it is a part, have been no less fortunate in their benefactors in the fine arts than in other fields. Although the bequest took effect in July 1978, it was not possible to exhibit the Princes Gate Collection until certain legal formalities had been completed. It was also necessary to find additional space to house temporarily those parts of the Courtauld Institute's collections, now so splendidly augmented, which have to be stored until some larger, permanent home could be found. The Home House Trustees and our Committee of Management felt that it would be most appropriate to show the Courtauld Collection and the Princes Gate Collection together at the Woburn Square Galleries for about a year, since it would not be possible, sadly, to continue to show the Gambier-Parry, Lee of Fareham, and Fry Collections in the restricted space available to us there. (Only the Lee of Fareham Rubens *Descent from the Cross* has been included, since it relates to Rubens' *Visitation* and *Presentation* in the Princes Gate Collection.) This underlines our need for more exhibition space where almost all the treasures in our collections can be publicly displayed. It is to be hoped that negotiations between the University and the Government, and the consultants' studies already initiated, will be successfully concluded and enable us to move the collections and, ultimately, the Courtauld Institute, to the Fine Rooms at Somerset House, thus re-uniting under one roof our teaching activities with the art collections.

The present exhibition contains all but a few of the paintings from Count Seilern's collection, and a selection of some sixty of the finest of the drawings. There will be two selections (A and B) of about thirty drawings each. They will each be shown for approximately six months at a time and both sections A and B are included in this catalogue.

An enterprise of this kind cannot be undertaken without financial help, and we wish to record our deep gratitude to National Westminster Bank for generously agreeing to sponsor this exhibition. We would also like to thank most warmly the Rt. Hon. Paul Channon, P.C., M.P., Minister for the Arts, for agreeing to a government indemnity for this exhibition.

The catalogue has been compiled by Mrs. Helen Braham, who assisted Count Seilern in cataloguing and curating his collection. The catalogue contains new information and references to books and articles published after the Princes Gate Collection catalogues appeared between 1955 and 1971. We thank her for undertaking the work of preparing this exhibition catalogue and for meeting cheerfully the exigent deadline set her. All exhibition catalogues are in the nature of progress reports, and this one is no exception. Mrs. Braham joins with us in thanking those of our colleagues who read entries for works which fell within their specialist fields and who made helpful contributions.

We wish to thank our colleagues at Senate House and in the technical services departments of the University, including our own Department of Technology and Conservation, our Photographic Department, Mr. William Bradford and Mr. William Clarke, without whose help this exhibition could not have been realised. Finally, we thank Mr. Gordon H. Roberton of A. C. Cooper Ltd and Mr. Graham Johnson and Mr. Tony Sumner of Lund Humphries for their essential help in the design and printing of this catalogue.

Peter Lasko
Director
Courtauld Institute of Art

Dennis Farr
Director
Courtauld Institute Galleries

July 1981

Introduction

The collection bequeathed by Count Antoine Seilern, at his death on 6 July 1978, to the Home House Trustees for the Courtauld Institute of Art, London University, is the fruitful result of nearly half a century of scholarship and acquisition. It comprises chiefly paintings and drawings, but also prints and a large art library, including rare books. Also forming a part until 1978, when they were bequeathed to various other private and public collections, were illuminated manuscripts, sculpture, coins and medals, Greek and Chinese antiquities (recently on loan to the British Museum), a further collection of prints, notably by Dürer, a few other paintings and a group of drawings chiefly of the 19th-century Austrian and German schools.

Outstanding among this wide-ranging assembly of works of art are the paintings and drawings which now form part of the Courtauld Collections. They span a period of over 600 years, from 1338 (Bernardo Daddi's *Triptych*, 14)* to 1950 (Kokoschka's *Triptych*, inv. no. 260 – not on exhibition on account of its size), and include works of most of the major European schools. The work of one particular artist, however, receives pronounced emphasis: Rubens is represented by twenty three drawings and thirty two paintings. By only one other artist is there a remotely comparable number of works: Giambattista Tiepolo's twelve paintings and over thirty drawings. All but one of these paintings are *modelli,* or oil sketches, as are at least twenty of Rubens' paintings.

The Flemish and Italian paintings and drawings are, indeed, by far the most numerous, each beginning with an important and particularly well-preserved triptych: the earliest known masterpiece of Netherlandish panel painting, by the Master of Flémalle (45) and Bernardo Daddi's altarpiece of 1338. Other early Flemish works include a drawing by Hugo van der Goes (167), a group of drawings (126–8, 155–6), notably landscapes, and two paintings (8, 9) by Pieter Bruegel the Elder, whose pictures are rare outside Vienna, and Quinten Massys' outstandingly well-preserved *Madonna* (44). From the 17th century – and apart from Rubens – there are chiefly works by Rubens' pupil, van Dyck, and by David Teniers the Younger, whose association with the collection of the Austrian Archduke Leopold Wilhelm made him of particular interest to Count Seilern: there are fourteen of his small copies (91–104) after paintings in the Archduke's collection, made for the production of his engraved catalogue, the first of its kind. Count Seilern's early attachment to the Kunsthistorisches Museum and his admiration for Archduke Leopold Wilhelm as the founder of its collections, led him to bequeath to Vienna two paintings (by van Dyck and Fetti, inv. nos.45 and 106) which had strayed long ago from the archducal holdings.

Of the Italian schools it is, with a few exceptions, notably the triptych of 1338, the 16th and 18th centuries which provide the two focal centres – and within these the Venetians in particular. In the 18th century Giambattista Tiepolo dominates; he is accompanied by, among others, his son Domenico (drawings), Guardi (a painting, 30, and fourteen drawings, 136), Sebastiano Ricci (57), Pittoni (52, 53) and Canaletto (two important drawings 129, 130). The 16th-century Venetians include Titian (121), Tintoretto (four

*Numbers in brackets refer to the catalogue entries of this exhibition. Inv. nos. refer to paintings listed in Appendices I and II. Drawings without reference numbers are not included in the present exhibitions A and B.

paintings, 117–120, and five drawings, 152), Palma Vecchio (48), Paris Bordone (6) and Lotto (an attributed drawing, 137, and three paintings, 37, 38, and one not on exhibition). Artists from other North Italian centres include Parmigianino (some twenty drawings, 140, 173–4, and two of his rare paintings, 49, 50). The Italian drawings of the period are by a wide range of artists, from many lesser-known ones to the greatest – Bellini (125), Mantegna (170), Leonardo (169) and no fewer than six sheets by Michelangelo (138–9, 171–2).

No English works of art are to be found here (a few drawings by Count Seilern's cousin, Lord Methuen, were formerly in the collection); only one minor Spanish painting (not on exhibition) and a Goya drawing; of the Germans only two small paintings (1, 33), but three drawings by Dürer (161–3). There is only one Dutch painting (32), but Rembrandt is represented by thirty drawings (142–5, 177–8). The French collection is larger and more varied, from Claude (one small painting, 11, and half a dozen drawings, 134, 158), through the 18th century – drawings, mainly by Watteau (nine; 153) but including also two Fragonards (135, 166) – to the 19th-century Barbizon painters, Diaz (18) and Daubigny (15), and the Impressionists: paintings by Pissarro (51), Manet (40), Berthe Morisot (46), Renoir (56), Degas (16, 17) and ending with Cézanne's late landscape (10). Drawings of the period include three by Cézanne (132–3, 157).

The 20th-century works are almost all Austrian and by personal friends of Count Seilern's, notably Oskar Kokoschka. His large *Triptych* was executed in 1950 as a ceiling painting for 56 Princes Gate, and was painted on the premises. These, and the many (uncatalogued) 19th-century Austrian drawings no longer with the collection, are evidence of Count Seilern's special affection for the art and culture of that country.

The breadth of the collection reflects a considerable catholicity of taste, but there is also a discernible pattern to its formation. The high quality and good condition of the majority of the works of art of all types are evidence of Count Seilern's connoisseurship; where quality or condition is relatively poor the reason may be either that it was acquired when he was still a novice, or it was bought as an act of kindness or charity, or because it was of historical interest. It is a collection of outstanding taste and the product of a love of fine works of art for their own sake. It is also a scholarly collection *par excellence*, and much of its interest derives from the relationship of works brought together here, often for the first time since the artist's death.

In the Rubens collection Count Seilern assembled three related *Conversions of S. Paul* – two paintings (68, 69) and a drawing (180), the latter having been acquired in two parts from different sources. Similarly, six oil sketches or *modelli* (72–77) are brought together here which were for Rubens' great series of ceiling paintings in the Jesuit church in Antwerp; there is also a set of 18th-century watercolour copies and a book of engravings recording this now lost series. Other interesting documents relating to Rubens include the MS. Inventory of his collection made at his death for the perusal of Charles I, the artist's last surviving autograph letter, and the transcript of a lost 'Pocketbook' of his sketches and notes ('MS. Johnson'). Another project at the heart of the collection is Tiepolo's last major commission, the altarpieces for Aranjuez in Spain, of which the five *modelli* (111–115), a drawing (184) and the fragment of an altarpiece (116) were assembled over the years.

It is worth remarking on the number of copies after the work of other artists, apart from the fourteen copies by Teniers: four of Rubens' paintings (58, 62, 78, 80) and a drawing are copies, or near copies – after Titian, Raphael, Elsheimer, Pordenone; the van Dyck bequeathed to the Kunsthistorisches Museum is after Titian. There are Delacroix and Watteau drawings after Rubens, a modern 'fantasy' by Frankl also after Rubens, drawings by the same artist of medieval sculpture and studies by Tintoretto after Michelangelo sculpture (152). A copy attributed to Hans von Aachen is after a Barocci altarpiece and Steenwyck's small copper is after an engraving by Theodor de Bry; there are studies after Italian masters attributed to Jordaens and others by 18th-century French draughtsmen.

The history of the collection began in the late 1920s, when the first few paintings and drawings were acquired. Count Seilern came relatively late in life to the study and collecting of works of art. Born in Frensham, Surrey, on 17 September 1901, he was the third son of the Austrian Count Carl Seilern und Aspang (1866–1940; he also had British nationality) and his American-born first wife, Antoinette Woerishoffer (1875–1901). His mother died at his birth. His father's second wife, Countess Ilse, was held in the greatest affection by her stepson. Among his Seilern ancestors were two Austrian Court Chancellors, the first of whom, Johann Friedrich (1645–1715), celebrated diplomatist and founder in 1684 of the titles of Seilern and Aspang, was the architect of the 'Pragmatic Sanctions', which ensured the succession of Maria Theresa and shaped the future course of the Austro-Hungarian monarchy. His nephew and adopted heir, Johann Friedrich II (1676–1751), became Maria Theresa's Chancellor; one of his sons, Christian August (1717–1801) was ambassador to England.

Count Seilern's mother's family was of German origin, some three generations back, and had made its mark on New York-German society. Wealth, derived from their successful and politically influential German-language New York newspaper, the liberal *New Yorker Staats-Zeitung*, had been munificently spent, though without display, on philanthropic charitable concerns and foundations. Three generations of remarkable and distinguished women included the youngest, Carola, sister to Antoinette, highly intelligent and well-educated, who died in 1911 at the age of 26, having spent her short adult life in dedicated social work. Carola and Antoinette's grandmother, Anna Uhl (née Behr), later Ottendorfer (1815–1884), had, with the aid of her second husband, built up both the family's fortune and, likewise, numerous large-scale but modestly-performed charities. Her daughter, Anna Woerishoffer (1850–1931), was Count Antoine Seilern's greatly loved and admired grandmother, with whom he spent some of his childhood in New York and Vienna. She, also, was a woman of great character, and held advanced views on social reform. She possessed a small collection of 19th-century paintings which were inherited in 1931 by her three grandsons. These are now largely dispersed, except for the Diaz (18) and Daubigny (15) in this collection, which are the only works inherited by Count Seilern; the rest were all purchased, with the exception of one or two gifts from friends.

Count Seilern dedicated the first of the seven volumes of his catalogue of the paintings and drawings to Anna Woerishoffer, and he wished this collection to be associated with her name. From her family, which Count Seilern recollected with pleasure, his characteristically reticent generosity surely derived.

Count Seilern shunned publicity and to a remarkable degree wished to dissociate his name from his many acts of generosity to art institutions and charities. These should not now remain unrecorded; least of all can those who have always associated him with the present collection forget that the bequest was his. Other gifts included a van Dyck portrait to the National Gallery at the end of the war and two panels by Michael Pacher to the Vienna collections in 1939 (now Oesterreichische Galerie). Numerous institutions received financial aid, including the National Art-Collections Fund and the National Trust, which jointly received the proceeds from the sale of his catalogue. Most magnificent was his anonymous gift in 1946 to the British Museum Print Room – to which he showed many other acts of generosity – of about 1,250 Old Master drawings, almost the entire Fenwick Collection, with the exception only of a few which he retained.

He did not wish to be seen as a public benefactor, but as the owner of what he always termed his 'little collection'. He deplored most of all the use of art as financial investment, and the correspondingly huge sums for which works of art now change hands; he also mourned the decline of the true private collection, and the monolithic scale of institutions which could, in his view, detract from the enjoyment of art, but he supported generously the museums he befriended.

His youth as a sportsman was revealed at Princes Gate by the numerous big game trophies which adorned the stairwell. In the 1920s and early 1930s Count Seilern travelled widely and adventurously in search of big game: to Africa (1926 and 1930), Mongolia (1930), Indochina (1931), Yukon (1932–3); he made a round-the-world voyage (1930–1); he qualified as a pilot; he bred and raced horses with enthusiasm and success, until the war. There were also brief ventures into training in forestry, engineering, business and banking, but the course of his career changed when he enrolled in 1933 at Vienna University. He studied, until 1937, philosophy, psychology (with the Freudian, Bühler), history, archaeology and, principally, art history (with Swoboda, Sedlmayr, Schlosser). It was then that he came under the benign and learned influence of Johannes Wilde, who was on the staff of the Kunsthistorisches Museum. His friendship with Wilde (who died in 1970) was of paramount importance to him throughout the remainder of his life, and indeed led, through Wilde's post-war Deputy Directorship of the Courtauld Institute of Art, to Count Seilern's friendship with this Institute and ultimately to the present bequest. After some years spent in the pursuit of pleasures typical of the time and his social milieu, Count Seilern became, gradually, so deeply and seriously immersed in the study and collecting of works of art as to be less at home with the Central European aristocracy from which he sprang than in the society of scholars and art lovers whose professional conversation most interested him.

One can to some extent trace the factors which influenced the style of the collection; the rise and decline of particular interests and the constancy of others can be detected by following the sequence of acquisitions. The Kunsthistorisches Museum was undoubtedly an impressive and constant source of pleasure and study, especially in the pre-war years. Much of his time was also spent studying art in Belgium and Italy, especially in Venice. For advice on acquisitions he turned, always, to Johannes Wilde, and in these years also, and especially for Rubens, to Ludwig Burchard (died 1960). The care of the collection was placed in the hands of the restorer at the Kunsthistorisches Museum, Sebastian Isepp, and remained so until the latter's death in 1954. Count Seilern came to depend also on the scholarly advice and the friendship of, in particular, Jan van Gelder and James Byam Shaw. His modesty and his respect for scholarship in others is evident in Count Seilern's post-war catalogue. Indeed, at his request the entries on Titian and Mantegna were written entirely by Wilde, the *addenda* to the *Flémalle Triptych* by Jan van Gelder, and all the entries on Claude by Michael Kitson. The entries on the Michelangelo drawings remained unwritten: Count Seilern waited in vain for Wilde to write them. New interests led to, and were perhaps encouraged by, friendship with scholars knowledgeable in that particular field. Certainly, unlike many collectors, he was always ready to relegate a work in his collection to a lesser artist if evidence pointed that way. The *Corrigenda* volume of the catalogue contains several such instances. Characteristically, he agreed with the view once expressed to him, "ownership is too close a bond". He read voraciously; even in the days of big game hunting his pack-mule would be laden with books. He visited when possible every exhibition of interest and recorded his opinions in the catalogues; he filled notebooks with accounts of works seen on his frequent travels and acquired an intimate knowledge of the great European public collections as well as many private ones.

By 1939 a substantial number of major works of art had already been acquired. On the brink of war, he was able to move to England with the contents from his house in Vienna, for by then he had relinquished his dual Austro-British nationality and was a British subject. His interests and acquisitions at this date are recorded in two works of scholarship: the unpublished dissertation on Venetian sources of Rubens' ceiling paintings, for which he was awarded a doctorate in 1939, and the catalogue of his paintings (though not the drawings) housed at 6 Brahmsplatz, Vienna IV, which he published in 1937.

The beginnings, in 1928–32, were more modest: a Lotto portrait in poor condition (inv. no.74, not on exhibition), a little Aertsen (2), the *Christ crowned with Thorns* by a follower of Bouts (7), two van Dycks (20; inv. no.45) and the only Spanish picture (inv. no.255). The only drawings were apparently the Pissarro and a number by Count Seilern's contemporaries, Béni Ferenczy and Gerhart Frankl.

Then, in 1933, the first Rubens paintings were bought (77, 88). One of these was a *modello* for the Jesuit church ceiling, the project related to the subject of his doctoral thesis. Also in that year Massys' *Madonna* entered the collection. A range of drawings were acquired, too, and in the next year were joined by the magnificent *Helena Fourment* (147) by Rubens, as well as one of the two grand Canalettos (130); the other (129) was acquired in the following year. From 1934 to 1938 one or two Tiepolo drawings were bought each year and the first two of the Aranjuez *modelli* (111, 113) in 1937. He bought a variety of paintings between 1934 and 1938, including Berthe Morisot, Palma Vecchio, Fetti, Guardi, Titian, van Dyck. Most important of all were the Rubens paintings: the *Landscape by Moonlight* (89) and the *modelli* for the wings of the Antwerp *Descent from the Cross* (64, 65) in 1935, his copies after Raphael's *Castiglione* (80) and Titian's *Charles V* (58), *Jan van Montfort* (85) and *The Death of Hippolytus* (67) in 1936, two more *modelli* for the Jesuit church (73, 76) in 1937/8 as well as other *modelli* (86, 87) and three large panels: the two from the *Achilles* series (81, 82) and the *Conversion of S. Paul* from the Munich Museum (69).

Among the drawings, a few by Rubens were added in these years, the first of the

Bruegels (*View of Antwerp*, 127) and the first Dürer (*The Wise Virgin*, 161) in 1936, the first Cézanne (*Armchair*, 132) and the first Rembrandt in 1937. The Rembrandt belonged to a group of seven drawings bought from Victor Koch. Further drawings by Austrian contemporaries, Ferenczy, Frankl and Wiegele, were also added. Interest in French 18th-century drawings is shown by nearly a dozen acquired at that time. Later this interest waned, though Watteau, with his obvious association with Rubens, he continued to admire. In the mid-thirties, also, the distinguished collection of Chinese bronzes and ceramics was started, largely with the help of Wolfgang Burchard.

Immediately on his arrival in this country, just before the outbreak of war, Count Seilern acquired the first of his two paintings by Pieter Bruegel the Elder (8) as well as the second Rubens landscape (83). He bought for the first time from Kokoschka, the three water-colour *Flower Pieces* (168), as well as further works by Ferenczy and Wiegele, and he continued to assist Austrian refugee artists and to acquire their works during the next critical decade. The number and quality of paintings, drawings – and illuminated manuscripts – bought during the first few years of the war is remarkable. Throughout, Count Seilern served in the army, first volunteering for the Finns' brief war against the Russians, which was over before he arrived. He returned to this country through occupied Norway and a wide arc of war-torn Europe and joined up as a gunner in the Royal Artillery. By the end of the war he was serving as an interpreter in Europe.

In the years 1940–42 he nevertheless managed to acquire notable works. Through the assistance of Jan van Gelder he bought in 1940 (and collected in Holland after the war) three Rubens oil sketches from the Koenigs collection, including that for the Whitehall ceiling (59, 68, 84), and in the same year bought the first Michelangelo drawing, the late *Crucifixion* (172). In 1941 acquisitions included the painting and two further drawings by Cézanne (133, 157), the largest Rubens painting, *The Brazen Serpent* from the Cook collection (61), and three drawings by him (146, 148), the small Degas (17) and van Dyck (23), the Pissarro and (in 1942) the Renoir landscape. To crown this, in 1942 he bought the beautiful 'Limbourg' Book of Hours and the hitherto totally unknown triptych by the Master of Flémalle, probably the most important single work in the collection.

There followed, not unexpectedly, a few years of quiescence in the growth of the collection. It was transported, with national collections, to the caves of Wales, where Johannes Wilde was among the custodians. Wilde's subsequent internment and deportation as an alien, in the heat of war, to Canada, caused great distress. Only one drawing, a Bruegel figure study (155), seems to have been acquired in the years 1943–44.

After the war Count Seilern moved to 56 Princes Gate, Kensington, and created there, with the assistance of the frame expert, Paul Levi, a setting for the collection, including a picture gallery for the Rubens paintings reminiscent of the gallery at 6 Brahmsplatz in pre-war Vienna. In 1945 the two finest *modelli* for Rubens' ceiling in Antwerp (74, 75) were acquired from the Cook collection, and in the following year the entire Fenwick collection of drawings. Count Seilern retained some two dozen of these, ten of which are miniature drawings by Stefano della Bella; others include a Bruegel landscape, the Carpaccio (131), the Leonardo (169) and six by Rubens (including the plant study, 181). There followed a continuous phase of collecting from the late 1940s until a few years before his death, diminishing somewhat as prices rose sharply in the 1960s, and of intensive scholarly study in preparation for the seven volumes of the catalogue published between 1955 and 1971.

His interest in 18th-century French drawings as well as 19th-century French paintings and drawings declined, although in 1954 he purchased Degas' exceptional *Lady with a Parasol*. He bought no more Cézannes, but this was a source of regret; Cézanne was the only artist of this school for whom Count Seilern retained a deep admiration. No 20th-century paintings or drawings followed after Kokoschka's *Prometheus Triptych* of 1950, although a number of his illustrated books and portfolios of lithographs were subsequently acquired.

Rubens' art remained a constant source of pleasure and inspiration for Count Seilern. The *Jan Brueghel Family* portrait (66) came in 1948 and further paintings were acquired in 1950 (*Sacrifice* after Elsheimer, 78), 1953 (*The Daughters of Cecrops*, 70, and *The Entombment*, 71), 1955 (*Cain and Abel*, 60), 1958 (*Coronation of the Virgin*, 72), 1959 (*The Annunciation*, 63) and 1960 (*Cortez*, 62). A dozen drawings by Rubens were also bought in the post-war years, as well as a number of works by van Dyck, including the *Man of Sorrows* (22) in 1967. Pieter Bruegel the Elder he constantly admired, and to the *Landscape* acquired in 1939 was added a newly-discovered *grisaille* painting (9) in 1952. Count Seilern was able to buy some half-dozen more landscape drawings by Bruegel, as well as figure drawings (the attribution of these is now controversial), in the late 1940s and 1950s.

His enthusiasm for G. B. Tiepolo continued, even increased. In 1949 two further *modelli* for Aranjuez (114, 115) were added, in the 1950s four paintings (105–6, 108, 116) followed, three more in the 1960s included the last of the Aranjuez *modelli* (112); the *S. Clement* (109), bought in 1970, was the latest painting to be acquired in the catalogued collection. On average at least one Tiepolo drawing a year continued to be added, sometimes as many as half a dozen; most were by Giambattista, but a few by Domenico. The majority of the drawings by Guardi were bought in the 1950s, although the only painting by him had entered the collection in 1935.

Just one small Rembrandt drawing had been bought before the war, but from 1947 and for the next twenty years one or more was purchased nearly every year, culminating in *Saskia, standing* (142) in 1962 and the *Seated Actor* (177), the last Rembrandt drawing to be acquired, in 1967.

Five Michelangelo drawings joined the first bought during the war: the outstanding *Dream of Human Life* (139) in 1952, three in 1963–4, including *Christ before Pilate* (171), and *The Virgin and Child* (138) among the last acquisitions, in 1970.

In 1951 the first of the small Teniers copies started the series of fourteen, the last added in 1970; two further copies in the series, acquired after 1970, are no longer with this collection. The work of Claude was also a post-war interest, the painting and some six drawings (134, 158) all bought between 1958 and 1962.

Among the 16th-century Italians the Titian had been acquired before the war; two Lottos (37–8) joined the first in 1949 and 1969; Tintoretto's four paintings and the drawings (152) were all bought between the late 1940s and early 1960s, Polidoro's two paintings and two drawings all in the 1960s, Fra Bartolommeo's nine drawings, including the seven landscapes (124, 154), between 1957 and 1961. Most significant, perhaps, of the post-war acquisitions representing Cinquecento art were the Parmigianinos. Twenty drawings were bought, beginning in 1953 with the beautiful *S. Mary Magdalene* (173) and continuing until 1970 (one or two drawings by the artist acquired later are no longer with the collection), and the two paintings were added in 1965 and 1966.

The rarity of some of the works bought in the 1950s and early 1960s should remind one of the element of chance in acquisition, such as two Dürer drawings (162–3) in 1954 and 1958, Hugo van der Goes' *Seated Saint* (167) in 1961, Bernardo Daddi's triptych in 1956. The preponderance of drawings, rather than paintings, acquired in the later years reflect, too, the dictates of rising prices and not unlimited funds. High costs and the scarcity of appropriate works of art on the market made it increasingly difficult for Count Seilern in the last years, burdened as he also was by failing health, to add to the collection. It would now be impossible to create a comparable one.

No collection on so ambitious a scale has been catalogued so scrupulously and devotedly by its owner. His other publications were few: one or two book reviews and articles, including one on *The Entombment* (71, then just acquired) in the 1953 special 'Rubens' issue of the *Burlington Magazine*, but the seven-volume catalogue of his much-loved collection is in itself a remarkable memorial to his scholarship.

Helen Braham

Publications by Antoine Seilern

Catalogues

Gemälde der Sammlung Graf Antoine Seilern, Vienna, 1937.

[A. S.] *Flemish Paintings and Drawings at 56 Princes Gate London SW7*, London, 1955 (I)

Italian Paintings and Drawings . . ., 1959 (II)

Paintings and Drawings of Continental Schools other than Flemish and Italian . . ., 1961 (III)

Flemish . . . Addenda, 1969 (IV)

Italian . . . Addenda, 1969 (V)

Recent Acquisitions . . ., 1971 (VI)

Corrigenda & Addenda to the Catalogue . . ., 1971

Periodicals

'An *Entombment* by Rubens', *Burlington Magazine*, XCV, 1953, pp.380f.

'Ein Fächer für Fürstin Eleonore Schwarzenberg von Karl Goebel', *Alte und Moderne Kunst*, V, 1/2, 1960, pp.10ff.

'Tiepolo Drawings at the Victoria and Albert Museum' (Review of G. Knox's *Catalogue*), *Burlington Magazine*, CIII, 1961, pp.71f.

Dissertation (unpublished)

Die venezianischen Voraussetzungen der Deckenmalerei des Peter Paul Rubens, University of Vienna, 1939.

PLATE I Bernardo Daddi *Triptych: The Virgin and Child Enthroned with Saints* cat.14

PLATE II Master of Flémalle (?Robert Campin) *Triptych: The Entombment* cat.45

The Catalogue

The present exhibition catalogue is based on Count Seilern's complete catalogue of 1955–71. Most of the entries are summarized, although it has been necessary in some places to expand the text, or to alter the emphasis. Some new suggestions have been added, many derived from recent publications, and a few titles have been changed. For reasons of space the reader is referred to Count Seilern's catalogue for literature published previously to the date of the *Addenda* volume (1971). Selected subsequent bibliography has been added, where possible or appropriate, to each entry here, together with one or two earlier references, notably to the 1937 catalogue of the collection. The list of exhibitions for each painting attempts to be complete; there are a few additions to the original lists. To the provenance of each work of art has been added the date and place of acquisition, previously not published. These dates are based on documents preserved among Count Seilern's papers. Most of the information in the *Introduction* has been pieced together from the same collection of documents, correspondence, newspaper cuttings and other mementos formerly preserved at 56 Princes Gate. A small collection of pamphlets and books record the more recent history of Count Seilern's family, as well as the celebrated 17th-century Imperial Chancellor Seilern. These include: *Carola Woerishoffer. Her Life and Work,* published by the Class of 1907 of Bryn Mawr College, 1912; *'In Memoriam'. Zur Errinnerung an Anna Ottendorfer. †1884*; Jossleyn Hennessy, *Some Seilern Memoirs,* 1974. A number of Count Seilern's friends have generously shared their memories of him. In particular I am indebted to Count Woldemar Schwerin for sending a vivid account of the adventures he shared with Count Seilern fifty years ago in China and Mongolia.

Finally I must record my gratitude to my colleagues, including those in the Department of Technology and Conservation, and principally to Michael Kitson for his encouragement from the early stages of this catalogue and to Dennis Farr for his generous understanding and support.

H. B.

Notes and Abbreviations

Artists are arranged in alphabetical order, and their works in an approximate chronological order.

Measurements are given in centimetres, height preceding width.

Dealers are, with some exceptions, not recorded in the provenances; where no vendor is given a sale is anonymous.

Place-names of exhibitions are only recorded when outside London.

Titles of exhibitions are generally shortened.

Paintings

1

Hans von Aachen(?) (1552–1615)

1 *The Entombment (after Federico Barocci)*

Copper. 30·6×21·5
Inv. no.249

Barocci's *Entombment* of 1582 in Senigállia was so much copied in the succeeding years that the artist had to repair the damage inflicted. The German artist to whom the present copy is attributed is reputed to have made numerous small copies of Italian masterpieces on his travels in Italy and was certainly influenced by Barocci's *Entombment* in his own work.

PROV. Sale, Christie's, 26 Nov. 1948 (176, as by Lambert Lombard). Acquired London 1948.

Pieter Aertsen (1508–1575)

2 *The Annunciation* (recto); *Christ Bearing the Cross* (verso)

Panel. 16×12
Inv. no.4

Six similar panels (present whereabouts unknown), forming part of a series which includes this, the only two-sided panel, and Number 3, were published by D. Kreidl in 1972 (see LIT.). The subjects are all from the lives of Christ and the Virgin. The existence of this two-sided panel suggests that the scenes were set in a winged altar; further panels would have completed the cycle, which must be among Aertsen's earliest works. The frame, inlaid with a variety of semi-precious

2 recto *2 verso*

stones, is Tuscan, early 17th century.

PROV. M. L. W.***, sold Galerie Fievez, Brussels, 18f. Dec. 1928 (7, as by Ambrosius Benson). Acquired Vienna 1929, as by The Master of the Prodigal Son.

EXH. Vienna Secession, 'Vlämische Kunst', 1930 (162).

LIT. *Catalogue* 1937, no.4; D. Kreidl in *Jahrbuch der Kunsthistorischen Sammlungen in Wien*, LXVIII, 1972, pp.59–62.

Pieter Aertsen (1508–1575)

3 *Christ on the Cross with the Virgin, S. John and S. Mary Magdalene and The Entombment in the Background*

Panel. 17·1×11·8
Inv. no.296

This small panel had always been attributed to Pedro Campaña until it joined this collection, when it was identified as being by Aertsen. It has now been shown to have belonged to a cycle of small panels (see under Number 2).

PROV. Acquired in Madrid by Sir Francis Cook; sold from Cook coll., Sotheby, 25 June 1958 (43). Acquired London 1959.

EXH. Burlington Fine Arts Club, 1908 (7); Grafton Galleries, Spanish exhibition, 1913–14 (28); Arcade Gallery, 'Italian and Spanish Paintings', 1958 (10).

LIT. See *Catalogue* IV; subsequently: D. Kreidl in *Jahrbuch der Kunsthistorischen Sammlungen in Wien*, LXVIII, 1972, pp.59–61.

Workshop of Fra Angelico (1387–1455)

4 *The Madonna and Child Enthroned between Two Saints (a Pope and S. Dominic)*

Panel. 15·4×9·9
Inv. no.70

The back of the panel, a private devotional picture, is marbled (but damaged) in dark colours similar to those used in the painting on the front. It was once considered to be by Fra Angelico himself, but the artist, although influenced by Fra Angelico, used a darker range of colours than is seen in the master's work, and is more interested in the decorative surface qualities of 'late Gothic', suggesting a date not later than the 1430s. The same artist seems to have painted the *Virgin and Child with Four Saints* in Bergamo (33×28; Accademia Carrara), where even the marbling in the foreground repeats the type found on the back of the present panel. Engraved as Fra Angelico by F. Bartoccini in Dennistoun's *Memoirs of the Dukes of Urbino*, II, 1851, when in the author's collection.

PROV. Gerini coll., Florence; James Dennistoun (1803–55), sold Christie's, 14 June 1855 (4); Sir John Ramsden; Capt. Norman Colville, 1936. Acquired London 1954.

EXH. Burlington Fine Arts Club, 'Gothic Art in Europe', 1936 (34).

LIT. See *Catalogue* II and *Addenda*; subsequently: H. Brigstocke in *Connoisseur*, CXCVIII, 1978, pp.317f.

5

6

Jean Barbault (1718–1762)

5 *Italian Landscape*

Canvas. 74×98·5
Signed and dated, lower left, 'Barbault, Roma, 1749'
Inv. no.201

The earliest of the few landscapes by Barbault so far traced, painted soon after his arrival in Rome. The artist is better known for his small figure paintings and his engraved views of Rome in the style of Piranesi.

PROV. Acquired London 1951.

LIT. N. Volle and P. Rosenberg in exh. cat., *Jean Barbault*, Beauvais/Angers/Valence, 1974–5, pp.14, 56f. (46); P. Rosenberg in *Piranèse et les Français*, 1978, p.502.

Paris Bordone (1500–1571)

6 *The Rest on the Flight into Egypt*

Canvas, transferred from panel. 48·7×68·8
Inv. no.75

A damaged and heavily overpainted picture. X-rays reveal, in addition, considerable alterations by the artist, particularly in the group of the Holy Family, where two heads in alternative poses can be seen to right and left of the Virgin, and more voluminous drapery. The tree was originally sparse in outline; its additional foliage may or may not be the artist's own work. Cautiously, bearing its condition in mind, it can be considered a very early, Giorgionesque work of the 1520s. Bordone was born in Treviso but spent most of his life in Venice.

PROV. Potocki coll., Cracow (1937 cat. no.6 (83)). Acquired from Count Adam Potocki 1951.

LIT. See *Catalogue* II and *Addenda*.

7

Follower of Dieric Bouts

7 *Christ Crowned with Thorns*

Panel. 31×21·5

Inv. no.2

One of a large number of paintings of this subject from the circle of Bouts, many of which are joined with the *Mater Dolorosa* to form a diptych. Christ is shown with a similar type of face in Bouts' major altarpiece, *The Last Supper* in Louvain, of 1464–67.

PROV. Inscriptions on the back indicate an unidentified (?)19th cent. Italian collection, no.8. Acquired Berlin 1929.

EXH. Vienna Secession, 'Vlämische Kunst', 1930 (30).

LIT. See *Catalogue* I; also: *Catalogue* 1937, no.1.

Pieter Bruegel the Elder (*c.*1525/30–1569)

8 *Landscape with the Flight into Egypt*

Panel. 37·2×55·5   COLOUR PLATE VII

Signed and dated, lower right, 'BRVEGEL MDLXIII' (very indistinct, especially the last two figures).

Inv. no.5

The mountainous landscape, in *Weltlandschaft* tradition, recalls Bruegel's alpine drawings (cf. Number 126) and series of engravings of the previous decade. The falling idol on the willow in the right foreground symbolizes the defeat of paganism by the coming of Christ; two microscopic salamanders – symbols of evil – can be seen below the passing Holy Family. This is the only known surviving painting by Bruegel which can certainly be traced to the celebrated collection of

8

Cardinal de Granvella, his great admirer and patron. At the time it was painted Granvella was Archbishop of Malines and President of the Netherlands Council of State. In the following century this painting belonged to the two greatest Bruegel collectors of Antwerp, first to Rubens, who owned ten or eleven others, and after his death to Pieter Stevens, who owned ten others, including the following painting.

PROV. Cardinal Antoine Perrenot de Granvella (1517–86); inventory of his heirs, Besançon, 1607; Sir P. P. Rubens, inventory after death (191); Senator Pieter Stevens, sold Antwerp, 13ff. Aug. 1668 (16); Diego Duarte, inventory after death, 1682 (72); William Neale, sold by Edwards at Tom's Coffee House, Cornhill, 14 Dec. 1803 (22). Mrs. Frank Holbrooke, sold Christie's, 14 July 1939 (86). Acquired at sale.

EXH. R.A., 'Flemish Art', 1953 (313).

LIT. See *Catalogue* I and *Addenda*; also: W. Stechow, *Pieter Bruegel the Elder* (1969), pp.19–22, 36, 155; subsequently: F. Grossmann, *Pieter Bruegel. The Paintings*, 3rd edit., 1973, pp.27, 30, 194f.; M. J. Friedländer, *Early Netherlandish Painting*, XIV (new English edit.), 1976, p.47, addenda no.52; M. Gibson, *Bruegel*, 1980, pp.15, 63f., 179; exh. cat., *Bruegel, une dynastie de peintres*, Brussels, Palais des Beaux-Arts, 1980, pp.33, 35, 70; J. Briels in *Jaarboek van het Koninklijk Museum voor schone Kunsten, Antwerpen*, 1980, p.206.

Pieter Bruegel the Elder (*c*.1525/30–1569)

9 *Christel and the Woman taken in Adultery*

9

Panel. 24·1×34·4   COLOUR PLATE VI
Signed and dated, lower left, 'BRVEGEL.M.D.LXV'; the inscription on the ground reads: 'DIE SONDER SONDE IS / DIE' (Flemish text, *John*, VIII, 7: 'He that is without sin among you, let him [first cast a stone at her'])
Inv. no.6

Along all four edges are pricks at regular intervals apparently made with compass points to aid the engraver, Paul Perret (engraving of 1579, not reversed). *Grisaille* paintings are rare among Bruegel's works: *The Death of the Virgin* at Upton House is the most notable other example. The subject appears to signify a deeply-felt plea for religious tolerance; the artist kept this painting for himself and it was apparently the only one inherited by his son, Jan Brueghel the Elder. The iconographic scheme is Flemish, but the austere composition and monumental figures are perhaps the most Italianate in all Bruegel's paintings. A copy in Bergamo (Accademia Carrara) could be the one made for Cardinal Borromeo when he returned the *grisaille* to the Brueghel family; there are a number of copies attributed to, or by, Jan Brueghel and Pieter Brueghel the Younger, some in colour and apparently made from the engraving.

PROV. Inherited from the artist by Jan Brueghel the Elder; bequeathed 1625 to Cardinal Federigo Borromeo; returned by him to Jan Brueghel the Younger; Senator Pieter Stevens, sold Antwerp, 13ff. Aug. 1668 (14); Henri van Halmale, Bishop of Ypres (1625–76); Hampden coll. from 18th cent.; Jane, Viscountess Hampden, sold Christie's, 19 Apr. 1834 (61); acquired by The Hon. Sir Alexander Hope; since then by descent; Major A. P. J. Hope, sold Christie's, 1 Feb. 1952 (60). Acquired at sale.

LIT. See *Catalogue* I and *Addenda*; also: W. Stechow, *Pieter Bruegel the Elder* (1969), pp.22f., 25, 92, 155; subsequently: F. Grossmann in *Album Amicorum J. G. van*

Gelder, 1973, pp.151f.; F. Grossmann, *Pieter Bruegel. The Paintings*, 3rd edit., 1973, pp.41, 196; M. J. Friedländer, *Early Netherlandish Painting*, XIV (new English edit.), 1976, p.47, addenda no.53; K. Ertz, *Jan Brueghel der Ältere. Die Gemälde*, 1979, pp.459ff.; M. Gibson, *Bruegel*, 1980, pp.15, 117ff., 170, 179; exh. cat., *Bruegel, une dynastie de peintres*, Brussels, Palais des Beaux-Arts, 1980, pp.37, 146; J. Briels, *Jaarboek van het Koninklijk Museum voor schone Kunsten, Antwerpen*, 1980, p.206.

Robert Campin: see Master of Flémalle

Paul Cézanne (1839–1906)

10 *'Route Tournante'*

Canvas. 73×92
Unvarnished
Inv. no.209

COLOUR PLATE XVIII

10

Painted after 1900, during the last years of the artist's life. Much of the ground, now somewhat discoloured, is exposed. This picture, thinly painted and with subtle tonal gradations, is particularly interesting as an example of Cézanne's late technique. The view does not seem to correspond with any locality known through other paintings of the period.

PROV. A. Vollard, Paris. Acquired 1941 from Sir Kenneth Clark.

LIT. See *Catalogue* III; subsequently: A. Gatto and S. Orienti, *L'Opera completa di Cézanne*, 1970, pp.118–9 (720, as Venturi 1532).

Claude Gellée, called Claude Lorrain (1600–1682)

11 *Landscape with an Imaginary View of Tivoli*

Copper. 21·6×25·8
Signed and dated, lower left, 'CLAVDIO(?) 1642'
Inv. no.413

In this small copper, painted perhaps as a souvenir for a departing traveller, the principal landmarks of Tivoli are rearranged to create a picturesque effect, and the dome of S. Peter's, Rome, is sited on the horizon. The horseman crossing the bridge is one of the last figures in contemporary dress which Claude painted – in later paintings his figures wear dress appropriate to pastoral, biblical or mythological themes. This landscape was recorded by Claude with great accuracy in drawing no.67 of his *Liber Veritatis*, but without the usual naming of the patron. An inscription in another hand connects it with Sir Robert Gayer (*c*.1639–1702), in Rome 1659–60. It appears, however, that he may have owned not Number 11, but a larger variant – probably not by Claude – now at Petworth. The present painting is among the smallest coppers by Claude, of which some fifteen are known.

PROV. (?) Sir Robert Gayer (*c*.1639–1702); France in mid-18th cent. (no.64 in sale(?) cat. cutting, formerly pasted on back of frame); Sale, Christie's, 13 May 1960 (168). Acquired London 1960.

EXH. Arts Council, Hayward Gallery, 'Claude Lorrain', 1969 (16).

LIT. See *Catalogue* VI; subsequently: M. Roethlisberger and D. Cecchi, *Tout l'oeuvre peint de Claude Lorrain*, 1977, no.131; M. Kitson, *Claude Lorrain: Liber Veritatis*, 1978, p.93.

11

12

Gaspar de Crayer (1584-1669)

12 *The Triumph of Scipio Africanus*

Panel. 35·5×26·9
Inv. no.34

This *modello* – now identified as by de Crayer, but formerly attributed to Rubens, and influenced by his *Triumphal Entry of Henry IV into Paris* – was for a scene on the *Arcus Caroli*, erected for the temporary decorations for the ceremonial entry of Cardinal Infante Ferdinand into Ghent, 28 Jan. 1635. The classical scene alludes to the modern triumphs of Charles V; it was engraved by J. Neeffs in G. Becanus, *Serenissimi Principis Ferdinandi . . . Triomphalis Introitus in . . . Gandavim*, 1636.

PROV. D. G. Drysdale, Bancroft. Acquired London 1947.

EXH. Colnaghi, 'Old Masters', 1947 (16).

LIT. See *Addenda*; subsequently: H. Vlieghe, *Gaspar de Crayer*, 1972, pp.38, 122 (A52); *Corpus Rubenianum*, XVI, J. R. Martin, *The Decorations for the Pompa Introitus Ferdinandi*, 1972, p.160 n.; J. S. Held, *The Oil Sketches of Peter Paul Rubens*, 1980, under no.83.

13

Giuseppe Maria Crespi (1665–1747)

13 *The Virgin with the Instruments of the Passion*

Copper. 22×16·8
Inv. no.110

Possibly the 'copper' of a 'vergine addolorata' in the choir of S. Omobono in Bologna, mentioned by Crespi's son Luigi (1769). Guido Reni, like Crespi a native of Bologna, had popularized the subject of the 'addolorata', but the unusual presentation of the instruments of the Passion may have been inspired by Rembrandt's etching (Münz, 234). Previously dated not later than 1720, the painting has recently been dated to *c.*1730.

PROV. A. Busiri-Vici, Rome, in 1948. Acquired New York 1955.

EXH. Bologna, Salone del Podestà – Milan, Castello Sforzesco, 'G, M. Crespi', 1948 (47).

LIT. Mira Pajes Merriman, *Giuseppe Maria Crespi*, 1980, p.253 (62).

Bernardo Daddi (recorded from 1312, died 1348)

14 *Triptych: The Virgin and Child Enthroned with Saints* (centre);
The Nativity; The Crucifixion (inside of wings);
The Adoration of the Magi (outside)

Panel. Total height: 87·5;
width at base: 42; wings: 62×17   COLOUR PLATE I
Dated 1338 on base: '·ANNO·D̄N̄I[M]·CCC·XXXVIII' (the central part of the inscription covered by an indistinct coat-of-arms, apparently added later)
Collalto family seal on back
Inv. no.69

This triptych has been preserved in a state of completeness and excellence of condition rare for its date. There are a few areas of slight damage and the finials above the twisted columns are lost, but much of the triptych, including the gold and its decorative punch marks, appears barely touched by wear. It is, moreover, an outstanding example of a type of small tabernacle for private devotion popularized by Daddi, one of the major Trecento artists, next to Giotto, working in Florence before the Black Death. It illustrates well Daddi's distinctive fusion of the styles of Giotto and Simone Martini, his narrative skill and inventiveness of detail and general design. The quality of execution is such that only the evangelists in the spandrels of the inner wings, and the two holy Bishops at the top of the outer wings could be ascribed to Daddi's workshop assistants, who are otherwise held responsible for much of the work on many comparable tabernacles. A triptych by Daddi in the National Gallery of Scotland appears also to be dated 1338. The central scene of Number 14 shows the Madonna and Child enthroned with Angels and Saints (left: John the Baptist, Francis, Dorothy and Lucy; right: Paul, Peter, Margaret and Catherine). The inner wings show the Nativity with the angel appearing to the shepherds, and the Crucifixion (with (?)Longinus wearing the hexagonal nimbus); the Annunciation takes place across the upper span of the opened wings. The Adoration of the Kings on the outer wings is presented in a scene continuous across both panels when closed.

PROV. General Count Ramboldo Collalto (1575–1630, born Mantua); by descent. Acquired 1956 from Prince Oktavian Collalto, Italy.

EXH. Brno Museum, Czechoslovakia (on loan, 1914–?); R.A., 'Italian Art', 1960 (266).

14

14 The triptych closed

15

LIT. See *Catalogue* II and *Addenda*; also: M. Levey in *Burlington Magazine,* CII, 1960, p.123; subsequently: H. Wagner, *Sammlungskataloge des Berner Kunstmuseums,* I. *Italienischer Malerei 13. bis 16. Jahrhundert,* 1974, pp.47, 50; R. Fremantle, *Florentine Gothic Painters,* 1975, pp.47, 57f.; H. Brigstocke, *Italian and Spanish Paintings in the National Gallery of Scotland,* 1978, p.37.

Charles-François Daubigny (1817–1878)

15 *A Landscape with a River*

Panel. 28×58
Signed and dated, lower left, 'Daubigny 1860'
Inv. no.204

The river is almost certainly the Oise, near the artist's home at Auvers. Daubigny painted a great number of similar views; the present riverscape most closely resembles those showing l'Ile de Vaux (see especially R. Hellebranth, *Charles-François Daubigny,* 1976, in which the present picture is not listed).

PROV. Mrs. Anna Woerishoffer, New York. Inherited 1931.

LIT. *Catalogue* 1937, no.26.

Edgar Degas (1834–1917)

16 *Lady with a Parasol*

16

Canvas. 75·5×85
Unfinished and unvarnished
Stamped signature of the Degas sale, lower right
Inv. no.207

COLOUR PLATE XVII

Painted probably 1870–72, the *Lady with a Parasol* can be compared with Degas' *Femme à la fenêtre* in the Courtauld Collection, which shows the same preoccupation with the effects of *contre-jour*. The small painting, *At the Racecourse* (E. Thaw, New York), has a subject and composition close to the present painting.

PROV. Contents of artist's studio, 2nd sale, G. Petit, Paris, 11ff Dec. 1918 (36); Marcel Guérin, Paris, in 1923. Acquired Paris 1954.

17

EXH. Paris, Gal. Charpentier, 1944–5 (45).

LIT. See *Catalogue* III; subsequently: R. Pickvance and J. Pečírka, *Drawings. Edgar Degas*, 2nd edit., 1969, p.25 (32); F. Russoli, *L'Opera Completa di Degas*, 1970, p.107 (439; as Lemoisne 414).

Edgar Degas (1834–1917)

17 *A Dancer ('Danseuse en Scène')*

Oil on silk. 23·5×13·5
Signed bottom centre, 'Degas.'
Inv. no.208

Painted probably in the late 1870s. Two drawings in the Degas sales (1918–19; see *Catalogue*) appear to be studies for this small painting.

PROV. Percy Moore Turner. Acquired 1941 from Sir Kenneth Clark.

EXH. Paris, Gal. André Weil, 'Degas', 1939 (5).

LIT. See *Catalogue* III; subsequently: F. Russoli, *L'Opera completa di Degas*, 1970, p.111 (536, as Lemoisne 454).

Narcissé-Virgilio Diaz de la Peña (1807–1876)

18 *A Clearing in a Forest*

Panel. 39×57
Signed and dated, lower left, 'N.Diaz – 74 –'
Inv. no.203

A view characteristic of the Barbizon painter, Diaz. Among the number of similar landscapes a small sketch in Boston (Museum of Fine Arts) is particularly close.

PROV. Mrs. Anna Woerishoffer, New York. Inherited 1931.

LIT. *Catalogue* 1937, no.25.

18

19

Abraham van Diepenbeeck (1596–1675)

19 *S. Thomas Aquinas*

Panel. 25·5×12
Inv. no.42

The present sketch is for an engraving by Michael Natalis (1611–1668), one of a set of twenty saints. There is a version of Number 19 in the Museum, Valenciennes.

PROV. Cremer coll., Dortmund (1914 cat. no.309, as *S. Raymundus* by van Dyck); Wertheim sale, Berlin, 29 May 1929 (46; as Diepenbeeck). Acquired London 1952.

Sir Anthony van Dyck (1599–1641)

20 *The Adoration of the Shepherds*

Canvas. 111×161
Inv. no.43

Considered to be among the earliest paintings by van Dyck, *c.*1616–18, it already shows, in the borrowing of motifs, the influence of Rubens. As so often with van Dyck's earlier works, there is a slightly larger version of this painting (Potsdam, Sanssouci). A third version is in the collection of Manuel Amador Valente, Lisbon.

PROV. Sale, S. Hartveld Gall., Antwerp, 25 Jan. 1932 (58, attributed to Jordaens). Acquired Antwerp 1932.

LIT. See *Addenda*; also: *Catalogue* 1937, no.14.

20

21

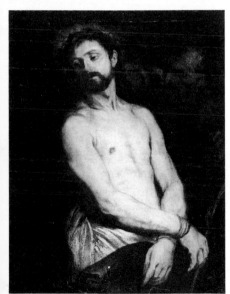

22 *recto*

Sir Anthony van Dyck (1599–1641)

21 *Portrait of a Man in an Armchair*

Panel. 120×81
Inv. no.44

Like the preceding painting, the present portrait is datable to van Dyck's earliest period, *c.*1616–18.

PROV. Lord Penrhyn, sold Sotheby, 3 Dec. 1924 (77; as by Rubens); ?Escher coll., Switzerland. Acquired Basle 1937.

LIT. See *Addenda*; also: *Catalogue 1937*, no.13.

Sir Anthony van Dyck (1599–1641)

22 *Man of Sorrows* (recto)

Oil on paper. 71×54

Studies for 'The Martyrdom of S. Sebastian' (verso)

Black and red chalk drawing. Not exhibited
Inv. no.302

A rare instance of van Dyck painting in oils on paper, this work has suffered on its *verso*, first from being attached to panel, and more recently from being covered with adhesive paper after being lifted from its support. The paper consists of two pages removed from a sketchbook, with a fold down the centre. The studies on the *verso* are for *S. Sebastian* (two versions: Chrysler Museum, Norfolk, U.S.A.; Alte Pinakothek, Munich), probably painted soon after van Dyck's arrival in Italy in 1621. The painting on the *recto* is linked with this project through the figure holding the robe around Christ's shoulders; a similar figure in *S. Sebastian* grasps the saint's head. The Titianesque *Man of Sorrows* probably dates from the same early years in Italy, as do a number of studies from Titian's paintings of the subject, in van Dyck's 'Italian Sketchbook' (British Museum). The *Man of Sorrows* in the Barber Institute of Fine Arts, Birmingham, appears to be a slightly later variant of Number 22.

PROV. Private coll., Genoa. Acquired Switzerland 1968.

LIT. M. Jaffé in *Studi di storia dell'arte in onore di Antonio Morassi*, 1971, pp.216ff.; J. R. Martin in *Proceedings of the American Philosophical Society*, CXXI, 3, 1977, pp.229ff.; J. R. Martin and G. Feigenbaum in exh. cat. *Van Dyck as Religious Artist*, Princeton Art Museum, 1979, pp.117, 124.

Sir Anthony van Dyck (1599–1641)

23 *Madonna and Child with a Bishop Donor and S. Anthony Abbot*

Panel. 18·8×22·2
Inv. no.46

The present *grisaille* sketch is presumably for a lost or unexecuted altarpiece, and probably dates from van Dyck's second period in Antwerp, 1628–32, when it became common for him to make small preparatory sketches. The inspiration of Titian, and notably of his *Pesaro Altarpiece*, is clear. Van Dyck's 'Italian Sketchbook' (*c.*1621–4; British Museum) contains a number of studies after Titian's

23

Madonnas, some closely comparable to the present sketch. The angel bearing the donor's mitre and pastoral staff may signify the celebration of his investiture. Three copies or variants are known.

PROV. Acquired London 1941.

LIT. See *Addenda*.

Sir Anthony van Dyck (1599–1641)

24 *The Crucifixion with S.Francis*

Panel. 50×36
Inv. no.303

A *grisaille modello* for Pieter de Bailliu's engraving (not published until 1643) after van Dyck's altarpiece (nearly 4m. high) now in the church of Notre Dame, Dendermonde. This, one of five large *Crucifixions* painted during van Dyck's second stay in Antwerp, 1628–32, was commissioned *c.*1629–30 by the Bishop of Ghent for the Capuchin church of Dendermonde, where it still hung in the 18th century. Van Dyck's authorship of Number 24, of which another *grisaille* version exists, has formerly been doubted, but now seems to be agreed.

PROV. ?Joseph Sousot, sold Brussels, 20 July 1739 (58); by 1931 Prince Franz Liechtenstein, Vienna (cat. no.102). Acquired London 1955.

LIT. See *Catalogue* IV.

24

PLATE III Quinten Massys *The Madonna Standing with the Child and Angels* cat.44

PLATE IV Palma Vecchio *Venus in a Landscape* cat.48

PLATE V Lorenzo Lotto *The Holy Family with S. Anne* cat.37

PLATE VI Pieter Bruegel the Elder *Christ and the Woman taken in Adultery* cat.9

Adam Elsheimer: see Koenig

Domenico Fetti (*c*.1588/9–1623)

25 *The Parable of the Sower of Tares*

Panel. 60·5×44
Inv. no.107

25

One of a series of fourteen known paintings by Fetti of the parables and sayings of Christ, the majority painted in more than one possibly autograph version. Number 25 may be the prime version; others are in Worcester Art Museum, Mass., Hradčany Castle, Prague, and G. Briganti coll., Rome. The series, perhaps initiated by the Gonzagas in Mantua, was apparently painted over a number of years; the present panel has been dated to *c*.1620–21. The parable (*Matthew*, XIII, 24–30) concerns the sowing of weeds ('tares') by the enemy, among the wheat, taken to allude to the spread of heresy in the Church. The 'Devil' in the painting is sowing in contrary conditions – left-handedly, across furrows, in a high wind. Another parable painting by Fetti, *The Return of the Prodigal Son*, was formerly in this collection (inv. no.106). It has been bequeathed to the Kunsthistorisches Museum, Vienna

PROV. Mrs. Ruth Spratting, sold anon. Christie's, 2 April 1948 (143). Acquired London 1951.

EXH. R.A., 'Italian Art', 1960 (391).

LIT. See *Catalogue* II and *Addenda*.

Domenico Fetti (*c*.1588/9–1623)

26 *Vertumnus and Pomona*

Copper. 18·9×26
Inv. no.108

COLOUR PLATE X

26

The story of the god and goddess of gardens and orchards is told by Ovid (*Metamorphoses*, XIV, 623ff.). Vertumnus, disguised as an old woman, courts the chaste Pomona, who has rejected all advances from her wooers – the putti, the distant statue of Diana and the herm of Silenus (right) allude to this. The tree supporting the vine is used as an allegory of love in Vertumnus' speech. He finally conquers only by casting off all disguise. This little copper, showing the influence of Venetian painting, is considered to date from the last two years of Fetti's brief life. He visited Venice in 1621 and from 1622 until his death. Its exceptionally small size and the use of copper set the present painting apart from other comparable works (a group in Vienna, Kunsthistorisches Museum). An attribution to Johann Liss has been proposed; more probably, it could be a type of painting by Fetti to influence Liss.

PROV. Acquired by the 4th Lord Methuen (1886–1975), Corsham Court. Acquired from Dr. and Mrs. E. Sklarz, London, 1956.

EXH. R.A., 'Italian Art', 1960 (392).

LIT. See *Catalogue* II and *Addenda*.

27

Flémalle: see Master of Flémalle

Flemish Artist, Mid-Sixteenth Century

27 *Landscape with S. Onuphrius (?) praying*

Panel. 16·6×19·3. Probably cut down
Inscribed lower left, 'BRVEGEL 156(8?)'
Inv. no.297

This little landscape, a picture in poor condition, presents problems of authorship and subject. The inscription, which resembles genuine signatures by Pieter
Bruegel the Elder (*c.*1525/30–1569), appears to be retouched, but cannot be
proved to be either genuine or faked. The painting does not fit stylistically into
Bruegel's latest period and a more likely attribution is to Herri met de Bles
(*c.*1480/90–*c.*1550). The hermit lacks S. Onuphrius' usual attributes of long hair
and a girdle of leaves.

PROV. Sale, Galerie Georges Giroux, Brussels, lf. Mar. 1957 (272). Acquired
1957.

LIT. See *Catalogue* IV.

Frans Franken the Younger (1581–1642) and David Teniers the Younger (1610–1690)

28 *The Interior of a Picture Gallery*

Panel. 58·5×79
Signed lower right, 'D.Teniers'
Inv. no.47

One of a number of unfinished paintings from Frans Franken the Younger's estate which Teniers apparently acquired and completed. His contribution appears to include the three foreground figures and three paintings on the chair in front, one of which is Jan van Eyck's *Cardinal Albergati* (Kunsthistorisches Museum, Vienna), once in the collection of Teniers' patron, Archduke Leopold Wilhelm. All these details are missing from an otherwise close version of Number 28 called *Intérieur chez Frans Franken* (Geneva, Museum). Two other pictures have been identified: *The Flight into Egypt*, by Frans Franken the Younger (Dresden), left, above the dog, and Aertgen van Leyden's *Nativity*, top centre, a version of which belonged to Frans Franken the Elder (died 1616), then to Rubens (a version in the Rubenshuis, Antwerp). The picture gallery seen here has recently been identified (see LIT., 1980; information from Dr. Lorne Campbell) as that of Pieter Stevens; he sold Van Eyck's *Albergati* to Archduke Leopold Wilhelm in 1648.

PROV. Sale, F. Müller & Co., Amsterdam, 1926; Sale, Lepke, Berlin, 24 May 1927 (147). Acquired 1934 from Professor Schindler, Vienna.

EXH. Vienna Secession, 'Vlämische Kunst', 1930 (119).

LIT. See *Catalogue* 1 and *Addenda*; also: *Catalogue* 1937, no.17; subsequently: E. Dhanens, *Hubert and Jan van Eyck*, 1980, pp.284, 286f.; J. Briels in *Jaarboek van het Koninklijk Museum voor schone Kunsten, Antwerpen*, 1980, pp.165ff.

28

29

Gerhart Frankl (1901–1965)

29 *Fantasia on a Picture by Rubens*

Canvas. 100×140
Signed and dated, upper right, 'GF 23'
Inv. no.262

A self-taught painter, apart from a brief period with the artists of Nötsch in Carinthia (see Number 122), Gerhart Frankl lived in England from 1938 until the year of his death. The present painting, an outstanding early work of 1923, was inspired by Rubens' *Landscape with a Thunderstorm: Jupiter and Mercury with Philemon and Baucis* in the Kunsthistorisches Museum, Vienna. It was the study of the works in that museum which was the main foundation of Frankl's art; two drawings in the present collection (inv. nos.286, 287) are after sculptures there.

PROV. Acquired from the artist 1947.

EXH. Vienna, Österreichische Galerie, 'Gerhart Frankl', 1962 (2); Salzburg, Gal. Welz, 'Gerhart Frankl', 1962 (2); Arts Council, Hayward Gallery, 'Gerhart Frankl', 1970–71 (1).

LIT. F. Novotny, *Gerhart Frankl*, 1973, pp.11ff., 35, 47f., 62 (69).

Gellée: see Claude

30

Francesco Guardi (1712–1793)

30 *Landscape – Capriccio*

Canvas. 46×34
Inv. no.113

This type of caprice landscape, suggestive of the islands of the Venetian lagoon, often showing (as here) a ruined triumphal arch, a temple beyond, and scattered figures digging (usually known as 'treasure seekers'), was a favourite theme with Guardi. At least three other paintings and two drawings (see LIT., Morassi) repeat closely the composition of the present painting, which has been dated to *c.*1780; there are numerous other variations on the theme.

PROV. A. Fauchier-Magnan, Paris, sold Sotheby, 4 Dec. 1935 (82). Acquired at sale.

LIT. See *Catalogue* II and *Addenda*; also: *Catalogue* 1937, no.24; subsequently: M. Levey, *National Gallery Catalogues. The 17th and 18th Century Italian Schools*, 1971, pp.127ff. under nos.2521, 2522; A. Morassi, *Guardi* (1973), pp.279, 485 (no.946), 486.

Italian, Early Seventeenth Century

31 *Portrait of a Man*

Canvas. 56·5×49·3
Dated on the left, 'Romae Añ 1612'
Inv. no.105

Attributions have been proposed for this portrait to Domenico Fetti (*c.*1588/9–1623) and to the lesser-known Ottavio Leoni (*c.*1578–1630) – the latter rejected in *Addenda*. If by Fetti, the portrait dates from the year before his departure for Mantua.

PROV. Acquired London 1951.

31

Lambert Jacobsz. (1592–1637)

32 *Abigail and Nabal*

Panel. 54·5×66·5
Inv. no.177

Abigail's drunken husband, Nabal, who has abused David, is in the background; in the foreground a servant is telling Abigail. She then makes her peace with David and after Nabal's death she becomes his wife. This rather obscure biblical subject (from 1 *Samuel*, xxv) is typical of the artist, who was also a Menonite preacher, born in Amsterdam and living chiefly in Leeuwarden. Certainly an admirer, copyist and collector of Rembrandt, he is reputed to have been to Italy and to have studied with Rubens. *Abigail and Nabal* corresponds in style with his later works.

PROV. English art market. Acquired Vienna 1935.

EXH. Leeuwarden, 'Lambert Jacobsz.', 1936 (8, as *Ruth and Boaz*).

LIT. See *Catalogue* III; also: *Catalogue* 1937, no.16.

32

33

Johann Koenig(?) (1586–1642)

33 *Latona changing the Lycian Peasants into Frogs (after Elsheimer?)*

Copper. 18·7×25·3
Inv. no.250

The story of Latona (Leto) taking revenge for being prevented, with her children, Apollo and Diana, from drinking from the lake is taken from Ovid, *Metamorphoses*, VI, 339ff. This painting has been attributed tentatively to Elsheimer, partly on the basis of an engraving by Magdalena de Passe which claims Elsheimer as 'inventor'; Elsheimer is certainly known to have painted the subject. More recently the present painting has been considered a copy after Elsheimer's lost original, perhaps by Johann Koenig, who was in Rome 1610–13; one of the Pynas brothers has also been suggested as the possible author.

PROV. Russian coll. ('Elueimer' [*sic*] in modern Russian script on back); A. Jaffé, Berlin. Acquired London 1950.

EXH. Berlin, Kaiser-Friedrich-Museums-Verein, 'Alte Meister aus Berliner Besitz', 1925 (105); Frankfurt a.M., Städelsches Kunstinstitut, 'Adam Elsheimer', 1966–7 (31).

LIT. See *Catalogue* III and *Addenda*; subsequently: M. Waddingham in *Burlington Magazine*, CXIV, 1972, p.610 n.; K. Andrews, *Adam Elsheimer*, 1977, p.166 (A2).

34

Oskar Kokoschka (1886–1980)

34 *Market in Tunis*

Canvas. 86×128
Inv. no.257

COLOUR PLATE XIX

The present painting, like the following one, was executed during a period when Kokoschka travelled widely; it is believed to have been started in Tunis in 1928 but not completed until 1929, in Asia Minor.

PROV. Marcell von Nemes, Munich. Acquired 1939/45.

EXH. Mannheim, Kunsthalle, 1931 (78); Paris, Gal. G. Petit, 1931 (35); Springfield (Mass.), Museum of Fine Arts, 'Modern German Art', 1939; Basle, Kunsthalle, 1947 (134); Zurich, Kunsthaus, 1947 (37); Arts Council Gallery, 'Austrian Painting and Sculpture 1900–1960', 1960 (75); Vienna, Österreichische Galerie, 'Oskar Kokoschka', 1971 (51).

LIT. See *Catalogue* III; subsequently: F. Novotny in *Bustan*, IX, 3–4, 1968, p.85.

Oskar Kokoschka (1886–1980)

35 *Landscape in Scotland (Findhorn River)*

Canvas. 71×91
Inv. no.258

Painted, like the preceding picture, during a period of extensive travels, this landscape was executed in 1929 during a tour of Scotland and Ireland. The river Findhorn runs near Inverness and Loch Ness. A painting of identical size,

35

36

Waterfall in Scotland – Findhorn River (private coll., U.S.A.), appeared with Number 35 in the two exhibitions of 1931 (see below).

PROV. Cassirer, Berlin. Acquired London 1941.

EXH. Mannheim, Kunsthalle, 1931 (80); Paris, Gal. G. Petit, 1931 (39).

LIT. See *Catalogue* III.

Oskar Kokoschka (1886–1980)

36 *Polperro*

Canvas. 57·5×80
Signed, lower right, 'OK'
Inv. no.259

Painted in 1939, this is the first of two versions in oil of the view of Polperro in Cornwall; the later version is in the Tate Gallery (No.5251). Of several known watercolours of the subject, one, a study for Number 36, is in this collection (inv. no.267).

PROV. Acquired 1940/46.

LIT. See *Catalogue* III; also: H. M. Wingler, *Oskar Kokoschka: The Work of the Painter*, 1958, no.317; subsequently: R. Alley, *Catalogue of the Tate Gallery's Collection of Modern Art,* 1981, pp.392f.

Oskar Kokoschka: see also Appendix I, inv. no.260

Bernardino Licinio: see Appendix I, inv. no.334

37

Lorenzo Lotto (*c.*1480–1556)

37 *The Holy Family with S. Anne*

Canvas. 58·5×78·9   COLOUR PLATE V
Signed and dated on the cushion, lower right, 'L.Loto [*sic*] 153. . (5?)'
Inv. no.73

A variant of this composition, in the Uffizi, is signed and dated 1534. Its chief difference is the presence of S. Jerome in place of the window with a landscape view on the left of the present picture. Differing opinions have been held about the order of execution of the two versions. A recent reading of the date on Number 37 suggested '1535', in which case it would be the later of the two. At this time (1530s) Lotto was resident in his native Venice but travelling frequently (1535 at Jesi). The image of the Virgin and Child seated on S. Anne's lap recalls Leonardo's cartoon in the National Gallery.

PROV. Acquired from A. Hoffmann, Vienna, 1949.

LIT. See *Catalogue* II; subsequently: R. Pallucchini and G. Mariani Canova, *L'Opera completa del Lotto*, 1975, p.115 (218); F. Caroli, *Lorenzo Lotto e la nascita della psicologia moderna*, 1980, p.272.

Lorenzo Lotto (*c.*1480–1556)

38 *The Entombment*

Canvas. 36·6×54·8
Inv. no.394

Generally agreed to be a very late work, *c.*1550, comparable in some details with *The Presentation in the Temple* at Loreto, where Lotto lived from 1552 in religious retirement, becoming a lay-brother in 1554. Religious intensity, as well as the uncertain hand of old age, are evident in *The Entombment*. There is a closely similar

38

version (private coll., Milan) and a preparatory drawing (A. Scharf coll.).

PROV. Private coll., Florence. Acquired Switzerland 1969.

LIT. See *Catalogue* VI; subsequently: R. Pallucchini and G. Mariani Canova, *L'Opera completa del Lotto*, 1975, p.121 (263); F. Caroli, *Lorenzo Lotto e la nascita della psicologia moderna*, 1980, p.290.

Lorenzo Lotto: see also Appendix I, inv. no.74

Alessandro Magnasco (1667–1749)

39 *Landscape with Washerwomen*

Canvas. 97·5×70·5
Inv. no.338

Formerly attributed to Marco Ricci. It was probably from Magnasco that Marco Ricci derived his wild and romantic style of landscape painting, which has its origins in Salvator Rosa. The washerwomen in this picture compete in popularity only with monks as inhabitants of Magnasco's landscapes, and there are numerous closely comparable works.

PROV. Sir W. W. Burrell, sold Christie's, 12 June 1897 (65; as Marco Ricci); F. M. Nichols. Acquired 1961 from Sir Philip Nichols.

39

40

Edouard Manet (1832–1883)

40 *'Marguerite de Conflans en Toilette de Bal'*

Canvas. 54×35·5
Inv. no.206

The sitter, who became Mme d'Angély, was a family friend; she was painted a number of times by Manet. The portrait has been dated variously to 1873 or 1875. It was photographed by Lochard in 1883 (no.86). Cleaned 1981.

PROV. Sale of contents of Manet's studio, 4f. Feb. 1884 (42), to Le Meilleur; private coll., Austria. Date of acquisition unknown, but before 1960.

LIT. See *Catalogue* III; subsequently: D. Rouart and D. Wildenstein, *Edouard Manet*, 1975, I, p.174 (205).

Follower of Andrea Mantegna

41 *The Entombment*

Miniature on vellum (showing wormholes); *verso* blank. 17·1×12
Inv. no.346

Formerly attached to the cover of John Walter's set of William Roscoe's *Works* (see PROV.) and removed in 1959. The miniature may have been a page cut from a devotional book. The central part is repeated closely in a *grisaille* on parchment (British Museum), cut on all sides and presumably once showing the entire scene. There are a few differences in small details, and the higher quality of the *grisaille* (though in poor condition) suggests that it is the earlier of the two. Another miniature of the *Entombment* (Cleveland, Ohio) appears to be by the same artist, who was clearly a late 15th-century follower of Andrea Mantegna, working perhaps in Verona or Venice.

41

42

43

PROV. Don Domenico Ricci, Treviso (?), c.1864; John Walter, sold Sotheby, 2 Feb. 1960 (249). Acquired London 1960.

EXH. Colnaghi, 'Old Master Drawings', 1960 (4).

LIT. See *Catalogue* V.

Follower of Andrea Mantegna

42 *The Man of Sorrows*

Tempera on linen. 42·3×30·3
Inv. no.330

This painting was at one time ascribed to Vincenzo Foppa (1427/30–1515/16), an attribution now rejected. The artist, as yet unidentified, was clearly working in the tradition of Mantegna, c.1500, perhaps in Lombardy. The head of Christ was once surrounded by rays, the background studded with stars and the edge of the garment decorated, all presumably in gold paint. These details were considered to be 19th-century additions and are now apparently overpainted, not removed by cleaning. It is possible that they are, in fact, reinforcements recording the original design.

PROV. Acquired London 1964.

Quinten Massys (1466–1530)

43 *Christ on the Cross, between the Virgin, S. John and Two Donors*

Panel. 50×34·5
Inv. no.295

Attributed formerly to both the young Gerard David (Benesch) and the young Massys (Friedländer, Winkler, Pächt), the present painting is now generally considered to be a very early work by Massys, from the early 1490s.

PROV. Lippmann coll., Berlin, sold Lepke, Berlin, 26f. Nov. 1912 (36); bought Artaria, Vienna; by 1931 Prince Franz Liechtenstein, Vienna (933; corresponding label with cat. number and coat-of-arms on the back). Acquired Amsterdam 1959.

LIT. See *Catalogue* IV; subsequently: A. de Bosque, *Quentin Metsys*, 1975, pp.127f; M. J. Friedländer, *Early Netherlandish Painting* (new English edit.), *Supplements* (1976), p.19.

Quinten Massys (1466–1530)

44 *The Madonna Standing with the Child and Angels*

Panel. 47·5×33   COLOUR PLATE III
Inv. no.3

Inscribed on the back of the throne which is being prepared for the Virgin, left background: 'B. Maria'

At one time the central panel of a silver-gilt jewelled altar with twelve tiny oval pictures set in the wings. This setting disappeared in the time of the Napoleonic Wars, but the painting is immaculately preserved. There are a number of possibly autograph versions of this composition, of which this appears to be the original, and that at Lyons is the best known. These are considered to belong to

44

45

the first years of the century, before Massys' great *S. Anne Altar* in Brussels, painted for Louvain in 1507–9. The type of the Madonna illustrates the revived popularity of the Van Eyckian Virgin of the previous century, while the putti with their garland are inspired by Italian Renaissance art.

PROV. Duchess of Holstein-Sonderburg (?); Count Philipp Sinzendorf by 1728; by descent through Sinzendorf and Thurn families (known as 'Memling' – see 1825 engraving by Peter Fendi). Acquired 1933 from Count Douglas Thurn-Valsassina, Carinthia.

EXH. Vienna, Kunsthistorisches Museum (on loan), 1932.

LIT. See *Catalogue* I and *Addenda*; also: *Catalogue* 1937, no.3; subsequently: M. J. Friedländer, *Early Netherlandish Painting*, VII, *Quentin Massys* (new English edit.), 1971, p.63, under no.27 (Suppl. no.165); A. de Bosque, *Quentin Metsys*, 1975, pp.15, 67, 113–6.

Master of Flémalle (? Robert Campin, *c.*1375–1444)

45 *Triptych: The Entombment* (centre panel); *The Two Thieves with the empty Cross and a Donor; The Resurrection* (wings)

Panel. centre: 60×48·9; each wing: 60×22·5   COLOUR PLATE II
Inv. no.1

In its original frame. Traces of paint apparently indicate the former existence of *grisaille* paintings on the backs of the wings. Otherwise excellently preserved.
Generally agreed to be the Master of Flémalle's first known major work, *c.*1410–20, and the earliest masterpiece of 15th-century Netherlandish panel painting. Nothing is known of the commission or the donor, and no inscription can now be read on his scroll, but the triptych may have been intended for a small funerary chapel. Celebrated for its originality of design and many innovations of detail, the altarpiece displays, alongside traces of the prevalent International Gothic style, a new realism and power. The only real precedent for this appears in the sculpture of Claus Sluter at Dijon, whose lost *Holy Sepulchre* may have inspired the central scene. In its complex symbolism the altarpiece appears to enshrine the

sacramental ceremonies of Holy Week. The donor, set in the mortal world, may also be interpreted as facing the hope of Eternity in the Resurrection wing, through Christ's sacrifice in the central panel. The wattle fence links the right wing to the centre; the donor is included in the central event by the glance of the angel on the left, one of four bearing the instruments of the Passion. Nicodemus supports Christ's head and Joseph of Arimathea the knees (a reversal of their more usual roles); the Virgin's Italianate appearance may be a reflection of Simone Martini's Passion polyptych then at Dijon (Champmol) (now dispersed; *Entombment* in Berlin – Dahlem); the figure between her and S. John appears to be S. Veronica (not generally shown at the Entombment); Mary Magdalene anoints the feet. Characters decorating garments appear to be Hebrew, but not forming comprehensible words. The raised plant designs in the sky, under gold leaf, are formed by gesso applied with a brush; they are varied in each panel for their symbolic significance.

PROV. Italian provenance indicated by 19th-cent. inscriptions on back (Mancinelli, no.32, Defalco(?), Colonna); Colonel R. F. W. Hill, Bickleigh, Devon, sold Christie's, 14 Aug. 1942 (13, as by Adriaen Isenbrandt). Acquired London 1942.

EXH. R.A., 'Flemish Art', 1953 (6).

LIT. See *Catalogue* I and *Addenda*; also: S. N. Blum, *Early Netherlandish Triptychs. A Study in Patronage*, 1969, pp.7–12, 117–9; subsequently: M. Davies, *Rogier van der Weyden*, 1972, pp.241, 254f; L. Campbell in *Burlington Magazine*, CXVI, 1974, pp.641 ff; B. G. Lane in *Art Bulletin*, LVII, 1, 1975, pp.21ff.

Berthe Morisot (1841–1895)

46 *Portrait of the Artist's Sister, Mme Edma Pontillon(?)*

Canvas. 56×46
Signed, upper left, 'B. Morisot'
Inv. no.210

The proposed identification of the sitter is based on known portraits of the artist's sister. Mme Heude has also been suggested. The portrait, dating probably from the early 1870s, may have been touched up by Manet.

PROV. Prague; Vienna, Gal. Miethke; 1904/1913, Baron Adolf Kohner, Budapest, sold Musée Ernst, Budapest, 26ff. Feb. 1934 (60). Acquired at sale.

EXH. Budapest, 'Maîtres de l'art français du XIXᵉ siècle', 1913; Budapest, Palais des Beaux-Arts, 'Oeuvres d'art socialisées', 1919; National Gallery, '19th-Century French Paintings', 1942 (21).

LIT. See *Catalogue* III and *Addenda;* also: *Catalogue* 1937, no.27.

Francesco de Mura (1696–1782)

47 *The Rest on the Flight into Egypt*

Canvas. 47×63
Inv. no.112

Considered to be a work of de Mura's early career, before his more mature 'Neoclassical' works, and certainly before 1740. In certain details this picture can be connected with a composition of the same subject known in two painted versions (University of Kansas Museum; D. Mahon coll.), but until recently only

46

47

known from the engraving of 1724 by B. Baron, inscribed as after Solimena, whose pupil de Mura was. The attribution to Solimena is now rejected. A version of Number 47 is in Dijon (Musée des Beaux-Arts).

PROV. Acquired Paris 1950.

EXH. R.A., 'Italian Art', 1960 (454).

LIT. M. Laclotte in *Revue du Louvre et des Musées de France*, 1962, XII, 1, p.266.

Palma Vecchio (*c.*1480–1528)

48 *Venus in a Landscape*

Canvas. 76×151 (including 9 cm. added to the top)　　COLOUR PLATE IV
Signed lower right, on a *cartellino* on the tree trunk, '(?). . . PALMA.P.' (much of the *cartellino* is now lost and the inscription may have been longer).
Inv. no.72

The addition (before 1934) to the top of the picture was intended as a replacement for a lost strip of canvas. It is generally assumed that this lost strip was of some depth, but unpublished X-rays indicate that the canvas was cut close to the original top of the picture. The landscape on the right is unfinished (X-rays reveal some alterations here) and this suggests a possible identification with one of two unfinished paintings of the subject listed as in Palma's possession at his death. The artist originally painted the head almost full-face, and glancing downwards, as the X-rays reveal. There are a number of paintings of the subject by Palma. That in the Norton Simon coll., California (formerly private coll., Sweden) appears to be a close version of the present one, to which a Cupid has been added, and the landscape completed in the style of Northern artists of the mid-16th century. Other versions of the subject are in Dresden and Cambridge (Fitzwilliam; a replica in Bucharest); in the latter, also including a Cupid, Venus

PLATE VII Pieter Bruegel the Elder *Landscape with the Flight into Egypt* cat.8

PLATE VIII Girolamo Francesco Maria Mazzola, called Parmigianino *The Holy Family* cat.49

PLATE IX Girolamo Francesco Maria Mazzola, called Parmigianino *The Virgin and Child* cat.50

PLATE X Domenico Fetti *Vertumnus and Pomona* cat.26

48

49

reclines in the reverse pose. Palma (Jacopo Nigreti) was a native of Bergamo, but settled early in Venice. The subject of Venus reclining in a landscape originated in Venice in Giorgione's *Dresden Venus, c.*1507–8; the present *Venus* may be dated *c.*1520.

PROV. Possibly in inventory at artist's death; Count Radetzky, Schloss Wetzdorf, Lower Austria. Acquired Vienna 1934.

LIT. See *Catalogue* II and *Addenda;* also: *Catalogue* 1937, no.19; subsequently: S. J. Freedberg, *Painting in Italy, 1500 to 1600*, 1971, p.495 n.21.

Girolamo Francesco Maria Mazzola, called Parmigianino (1503–1540)

49 *The Holy Family*

Panel. 43·1×47·3; sight size: 37·5×42·2;
unpainted border of *c.*2·7 on all sides
Inv. no.335

COLOUR PLATE VIII

The attribution of this painting to Parmigianino was at one period questioned but it is now generally accepted as a youthful work of *c.*1523, contemporary with his frescoes at Fontanellato and immediately preceding the artist's departure from Parma for Rome. In addition to the general dependence in style and mood on Correggio, the influence of Raphael may already be detected in the Child's pose, which the artist repeated closely in the *Holy Family* at Naples. A drawing in the Louvre (inv. no.6446) appears to be related; a copy of the painting is recorded as in Milan (Giolioli coll.); when in the Fries collection it was engraved by Agricola. On the back is an old attribution in German to Parmigianino.

PROV. Count Moritz Fries, Vienna, late 18th cent.; Freiherr Speck von Sternburg, Lützschena; Sir Thomas Lawrence, sold Christie's, 15 May 1830 (92); Miss Rogers by 1835; Samuel Rogers, sold Christie's, 28ff. April 1856 (559); Sir Francis Cook by 1868; sold from Cook coll., Christie's, 25 Nov. 1966 (63). Acquired at sale.

EXH. R.A., 1902 (189); Cambridge, Fitzwilliam Museum (on loan), 1947–58; London, Kenwood (on loan), 1958–64; R.A., 'Italian Art', 1960 (111); Manchester, City Art Gallery (on loan), 1964–6, and 'Between Renaissance and Baroque', 1965 (177).

50

LIT. See *Catalogue* V; subsequently: A. E. Popham, *Catalogue of the Drawings of Parmigianino*, 1971, under nos.6, 426, 823.

Girolamo Francesco Maria Mazzola, called Parmigianino (1503–1540)

50 *The Virgin and Child*

Panel. 63·5×50·7   COLOUR PLATE IX
Inv. no.336

Well-preserved but unfinished, most noticeably in the Virgin's drapery and lower right, where the ground is largely exposed. The architecture in the background resembles the later-demolished Septizonium in Rome. The painting, clearly influenced by Raphael and by Michelangelo, has been thought to date from the latter part of Parmigianino's stay in Rome (1524–7). A preparatory sketch in Vienna (Albertina) shows the Virgin with legs outstretched, as shown on the left of the present painting; a related etching by A. Quesnel after Parmigianino shows an alternative solution with both legs bent in an upright position; a drawing which appears to be a copy after Number 50 (Uffizi; inscribed 'Fran. Salviati') shows one leg outstretched thrown over one upright, as faintly indicated by the painting's *pentimenti*.

PROV. Acquired 1965 from Lord Kinnaird.

EXH. Colnaghi, 'Old Masters', 1965 (6).

LIT. See *Catalogue* V; subsequently: A. E. Popham, *Catalogue of the Drawings of Parmigianino*, 1971, under no.616; J. Byam Shaw, *Drawings by Old Masters at Christ Church, Oxford*, 1976, under no.1097.

51

Camille Pissarro (1830–1903)

51 *Festival at L'Hermitage ('Les Boutiques')*

Canvas. 44·5×53·3
Signed, lower left, 'Pissarro'.
Inv. no.205

This picture has been dated to *c*.1878. It was once entitled *Festival at Osny*, but was thought by the artist's son, Ludovic Rodo Pissarro, to show l'Hermitage at Pontoise, a place which appears in a number of Pissarro's paintings. The artist first moved to Pontoise in 1866, and spent most of the 1870s there.

PROV. Durand-Ruel, Paris; Cassirer, Berlin, 1913; Louis Ullstein, Berlin. Acquired London 1941.

LIT. See *Catalogue* III.

Giambattista Pittoni (1687–1767)

52 *The Holy Family*

Canvas. 70·9×55·9
Inv. no.339

Two closely similar autograph versions of this *Holy Family* are known (Quimper, Musée des Beaux-Arts; Zurich, Koetser); two further comparable paintings (Munich, Alte Pinakothek; Cordenans, Galvani coll.) are grouped with these and considered to date from the mid-1730s. A *ricordo* drawing of *S. Joseph* (Oxford, Ashmolean) appears to have served for that figure in all five paintings, as well as in the *Adoration* altarpiece of *c*.1739–40 (Brescia, SS. Nazaro e Celso).

PROV. Acquired Paris 1959.

LIT. F. Zava Boccazzi, *Pittoni: L'Opera completa*, 1979, no.89, and under nos.49, 96, 118, 163, 247, D4.

Giambattista Pittoni (1687–1767)

53 *The Adoration of the Shepherds*

Canvas on panel. 17×7·9
Inv. no.111

On the reverse the frame holds a replica of the original, by Sebastian Isepp (1884–1954).
A closely corresponding drawing by Pittoni forms a group with three others of similarly small size, arched format and related themes (all Venice, Correr). These have been considered to be models for either lost paintings or engravings – and dated variously to the 1720s and, with Number 53, *c*.1730–40. Recently, two paintings almost equally small (*Baptism of Christ; Last Supper;* 22·5×11·8 cm.; Lombardy, private coll.) have been connected with the four drawings and Number 53, and all considered to be independent works of *c*.1750–55.

PROV. Richard Buckle, sold Sotheby, 25 Apr. 1951 (93). Acquired at sale.

EXH. Arcade Gallery, 1943 (18).

LIT. See *Addenda*; subsequently: F. Zava Boccazzi, *Pittoni: L'Opera completa*, 1979, p.84, no.88, and under nos.71, 85f., D48.

Polidoro Caldara da Caravaggio (*c.*1490/1500–1543)

54 *The Incredulity of S. Thomas*

Panel. 202·5×124·5 (modern inset, lower left, *c.*74×34)
Inv. no.332

A very damaged painting, apparently not unfinished, with alterations by the artist now showing through clearly. Polidoro, at one time assistant to Raphael, was a productive artist, very little of whose painted work has survived – much of it adorned Roman palace façades. The artist's drawings form the best basis for the attribution of the present painting. It is identifiable with an *Incredulity* by Polidoro described in 1724 (F. Susinno, *Vite*. . .) as then in Palermo, formerly in Messina. Polidoro moved to Messina, *via* Naples, by 1534; the early 1530s has been proposed as the date of the painting. For its time the composition shows a marked originality; among the few comparable are Raphael's *Visitation* (Prado) and Michelangelo's lost design for the *Noli me Tangere* (realized by Pontormo).

PROV. San Tommaso, Messina, until 1707; Duke of Cesarò, Palermo (1724); S. H. Leroy Lewis, Kirkleatham Hall, Yorks.; Sale, Sotheby, 19 Nov. 1958 (121, as by Salviati). Acquired London 1963.

LIT. See *Catalogue* V and *Addenda*; subsequently: M. G. Ciardi Dupré and G. Chelazzi Dini, in *I Pittori Bergamaschi. Il Cinquecento*, II, 1976, p.308, no.10; L. Ravelli, *Polidoro Caldara da Caravaggio. I. Disegni di Polidoro. II. Copie da Polidoro*, 1978, p.149 under no.110.

Polidoro Caldara da Caravaggio(?) (*c.*1490/1500–1543)

55 *The Transfiguration*

55

Panel. 65·2×42
Inscribed on the tablet, lower left: 'EX GISULFORUM FAMILIA/EGO I PAULUS GISULFUS PER/M.AE.CAROLI V R. I./CĀCĒL.ITALICA PRE/FECTUS TABULA HANC/PRO ME ET MEIS P.(ingere) F.(eci)/ A(nno) R(eperato) S(?) VORN(?) MDXVIII'
Inv. no.333

This panel is close in style to three *modelli* in Naples (Capodimonte), which are firmly attributed to Polidoro, but because of the problems relating to it its authorship has been doubted. It may be the *modello* for Polidoro's altarpiece of the *Transfiguration* in Messina, destroyed by earthquake in 1908. The appearance of this altarpiece is not known, but may be recorded in Marco Pino's *Transfiguration* (Gesù Vecchio, Naples), which is closely related in composition to the present painting. Number 55, which shows alterations made during execution, appears to have been painted in the early 1540s, with some knowledge of Michelangelo's *Last Judgement*. Two drawings by Polidoro in the British Museum, together with further related drawings, are connected in subject and in the general design (derived ultimately from Raphael's *Transfiguration*, Vatican), and perhaps therefore with the same commission. The two tablets bearing the donor's portrait and the inscription do not appear in any other context nor in descriptions of the lost altarpiece. The inscription itself must record some earlier event: the date (1518, original and unaltered) cannot be reconciled with the style of the painting, and Charles did not become Emperor, as stated, until 1519. No record has yet been found of his Chancellor, the donor Paulo Gisulfo.

PROV. Hamilton Palace, sold Christie's, 17 June ff., 1882 (400, as by S. del Piombo); bought Nathan; Sale, Christie's, 1 April 1960 (102). Acquired at sale.

54

56

LIT. See *Catalogue* V and *Addenda*; subsequently: M. G. Ciardi Dupré and G. Chelazzi Dini, in *I Pittori Bergamaschi. Il Cinquecento*, II, 1976, p.308, no.11; L. Ravelli, *Polidoro Caldara da Caravaggio. I. Disegni di Polidoro. II. Copie da Polidoro*, 1978, p.185 under no.183.

Pierre-Auguste Renoir (1841–1919)

56 *The Outskirts of Pont-Aven*

Canvas. 55×65
Signed, lower left, 'Renoir'
Inv. no.211

A painting called *A View of Pont-Aven* (present whereabouts unknown) was like Number 56 also in Vollard's collection. Vollard recorded that Renoir's visit to Pont-Aven and his meeting there with Gauguin and de Haan took place in 1892. In that year, however, Gauguin was in Tahiti. The date of the meeting, and therefore presumably of the present landscape, was probably 1888.

PROV. A. Vollard, Paris; Capt. S. W. Sykes, Cambridge. Acquired London 1942.

EXH. Alex Reid & Lefevre, 'French Paintings of 19th and 20th Centuries', Aug. 1942 (8); Edinburgh and London, Arts Council, 'Renoir', 1953 (24).

LIT. See *Catalogue* III.

57

58

Sebastiano Ricci (1659–1734)

57 *The Adoration of the Kings*

Canvas on panel. 50·8×48·1
Inv. no.109

Closely related to the large canvas (*c*.3 m. square) in the Royal coll. (Hampton Court), Number 57 is considered to be either the *modello* or an autograph replica of the same date. The Hampton Court painting is dated 1726, one of a set of seven New Testament scenes by Ricci, commissioned or acquired by Consul Smith. The composition is clearly influenced by Veronese's *S. Silvestro Altarpiece* (London, National Gallery).

PROV. R. Matthews-Naper, sold Christie's, 15 May 1953 (29). Acquired at sale.

EXH. R.A., 'Italian Art', 1960 (447).

LIT. See *Catalogue* II and *Addenda*; also: M. Levey in *Burlington Magazine*, CII, 1960. p.123; subsequently: J. Daniels, *Sebastiano Ricci*, 1976, pp.52, 63 (195).

Sir Peter Paul Rubens (1577–1640)

58 *The Emperor Charles V (after Titian)*

Canvas. 75×55·5. Cut down
Inv. no.13

Rubens' copy is after Titian's equestrian portrait of *Charles V at Mühlberg* (Prado, Madrid), which he could have seen on his visits to the court of Spain in 1603 and 1628–9. There is some disagreement on the date of the copy, but 1603 seems more probable on grounds of style. An engraving of Number 58 by Theodor van Kessel (*c*.1620–after 1660) suggests that the portrait was originally waist-length, and broader. It can be seen in *Le Cabinet d'Amateur d'Antoine van Leyen* of 1671 by G. Coques (The Hague, Mauritshuis).

PROV. Probably no.79 (as by van Dyck) in inventory compiled after Rubens' death; probably Antoine van Leyen (1628–86), Antwerp; Prince Belosselsky, Russia, shortly before 1936. Acquired London 1936.

LIT. See *Catalogue* I and *Addenda*; also: *Catalogue* 1937, no.5; subsequently: M. Jaffé, *Rubens and Italy*, 1977, p.69.

Sir Peter Paul Rubens (1577–1640)

59 *S. Gregory the Great with SS. Maurus and Papianus;*
S. Domitilla with SS. Nereus and Achilleus

Panel. 61·5×46·5
Inv. no.14

This sketch is connected with Rubens' major Roman commission, the high altarpiece for S. Maria in Vallicella (the 'Chiesa Nuova'), 1606–8. The saints – mostly obscure – were specified for their association with the church and its Oratorian Fathers. The first altarpiece was a failure, due to the reflection of light, and Rubens substituted a tri-partite altarpiece on light-absorbing slate, still *in situ*. He brought the rejected version back to Antwerp late in 1608 and placed it in the church of St. Michael as a memorial to his mother. The present panel is now generally agreed to precede closely this first altarpiece (now in Grenoble), from

59

60

which it differs chiefly by being broader and less densely designed, and by omitting any indication of the miraculous image which was to be displayed above the saints. Recently, however, Held (see LIT., 1980) has considered the present sketch to be merely a reflection of Rubens' designs, by another hand.

PROV. London art market; Franz Koenigs, Haarlem. Acquired 1940 from the Koenigs coll.

EXH. Amsterdam, Goudstikker, 'Rubens', 1933 (14); Rotterdam, Boymans Museum, 'Koenigs coll.', 1935 (21); Brussels, Musée Royal des Beaux-Arts, 'Esquisses de Rubens', 1937 (24).

LIT. See *Catalogue I* and *Addenda;* also: J. Müller Hofstede in *Het Nederlands Kunsthistorisch Jaarboek*, XVII, 1966, pp.37, 59; subsequently: *Corpus Rubenianum*, VIII, H. Vlieghe, *Saints* II, 1973, pp.57f (109g); M. Jaffé, *Rubens and Italy*, 1977, p.97; J. Müller Hofstede in exh. cat., *Rubens*, Cologne, 1977, I, p.163; J. G. van Gelder in *Burlington Magazine*, CXX, 1978, pp.455f; J. S. Held, *The Oil Sketches of Peter Paul Rubens*, 1980, no.A33.

Sir Peter Paul Rubens (1577–1640)

60 *Cain slaying Abel*

Panel. 131·2×94·2
Inv. no.298

A painting from the time of Rubens' return to Antwerp from Italy, datable *c*.1608–9, shortly before the closely comparable Number 61 in this collection, *Cain slaying Abel* illustrates the interests and influences of that period. A number of Italian 16th-century sources have been proposed for the two figures – Michelangelo, Bandinelli, the Venetians – and the glimpse of landscape on the left is reminiscent of Elsheimer. There is a copy at Blois, and an engraving (not in reverse) by Buytewech of *c*.1612–13. A drawing by Rubens in Amsterdam (Historisch Museum) may be related.

PROV. 'M.B.', France, sold Paris, 20 f. Mar. 1827 (11). Acquired London 1955.

LIT. See *Catalogue* IV; subsequently: B. Heisner in *Southeastern College Art Conference Review*, IX (5), 1980, pp.211ff.

Sir Peter Paul Rubens (1577–1640)

61 *Moses and the Brazen Serpent*

Panel. 159×144. Original arched shape visible; additions to sides and top by the artist
Inv. no.15

Formerly attributed by some scholars to van Dyck, but now agreed to be by Rubens, painted shortly after his return from Italy to Antwerp in December 1608. A drawing by Rubens in the British Museum (see LIT., 1977 exh. cat.) contains studies apparently used for the present painting, which were derived from Michelangelo's *Brazen Serpent* on the ceiling of the Sistine Chapel. Rubens painted the same theme again towards the end of his life (National Gallery). The subject is from *Numbers*, XXI, 6–9.

PROV. Jaques Meyers, Rotterdam, sold Michel Bohm, Rotterdam, 9 Sept. 1722 (74, as by Rubens); Sir Francis Cook (as by van Dyck). Acquired 1941 from the Cook coll.

61

EXH. Antwerp, 'Van Dyck', 1899 (1, as by van Dyck); R.A., 'Seventeenth-Century Art', 1938 (76).

LIT. See *Catalogue* 1 and *Addenda*; subsequently: G. Martin, *National Gallery Catalogues. The Flemish School, c.1600–c.1900*, 1970, p.134; J. G. van Gelder in *Rotterdams Jaarboek*, 1974, p.175; J. Rowlands, *Rubens Drawings and Sketches*, British Museum, 1977, p.31.

62.

63

Sir Peter Paul Rubens (1577–1640)

62 *Hernan Cortez(?) (after Titian)*

Canvas. 97·5×76·5
Inv. no.299

This portrait appears to be a copy by Rubens after a now lost Titian, recorded only in bust-length format and identified by the engraver, Vertue, in 1724, as a portrait of Hernan Cortez (1485–1547). Titian cannot have met Cortez; his portrait, painted probably about the time of the explorer's death, may have been based, in its turn, on the authentic likeness sent by Cortez to the celebrated *Musaeum* of the Bishop Paolo Jovio, on Lake Como. This, too, is lost, but is recorded in a copy by C. dell'Altissimo (Pitti) and a woodcut by T. Stimmer. It has been suggested (see LIT.) that Rubens' original was not by Titian, but by Anthonis Mor. The present painting has been dated on grounds of style to *c.*1608–12.

PROV. Acquired London 1960.

LIT. H. G. Wethey, *The Paintings of Titian*, II. *The Portraits*, 1971, p.159.

Sir Peter Paul Rubens(?) (1577–1640)

63 *The Annunciation of the Virgin's Death (The Angel bearing a Palm from Paradise)* (?)

Panel. 92×74·3
Inv. no.300

The unusual subject tentatively suggested in the title is indicated by the palm carried by the angel instead of a lily, and by the Virgin's black veil and her prominent girdle (associated with the Assumption). However, when the composition was engraved by F. Luycx the inscription identified it clearly with the first Annunciation. It has been proposed that Luycx himself was the author of the composition, as Rubens' name does not appear on the print until the second state, but an attribution to Rubens, *c.*1609–12, has also been considered probable. There is a version (*modello?*) less than half the size of the present picture, and closer to Luycx's print, in the National Gallery, Prague.

PROV. A church in France. Acquired Paris 1959.

LIT. J. S. Held, *The Oil Sketches of Peter Paul Rubens*, 1980, under no.317A (as probably largely studio work).

64

65

Sir Peter Paul Rubens (1577–1640)

64 *The Visitation*

Panel. 83×30·5
Inv. no.16

65 *The Presentation in the Temple*

Panel. 82·5×30·5
Inv. no.17

Numbers 64 and 65 are *modelli* for the insides of the wings of the great triptych of

66

The Descent from the Cross in Antwerp Cathedral, commissioned in 1611 by the Guild of the Arquebusiers. The theme of the triptych is 'Christ-bearing' and Salvation, in allusion to the Guild's patron saint, Christopher, who is shown on the exterior of the wings. Among the other surviving preparatory works for this commission are a study for *The Presentation* in this collection (inv. no.56) and the *modello* for the central *Descent from the Cross* in the Courtauld Collections (Lee coll.). The differences in colour, scale and character of the Lee *modello* may be accounted for by the central panel being finished in 1612, the wings in 1614. The *modello* for *S. Christopher* (Munich) resembles Numbers 64 and 65, rather than the Lee *modello*. There are a number of changes between the present *modelli* and the altarpiece, and also during the execution of the *modelli*, where the alterations in the upper parts are now partially visible. Unpublished X-rays show considerable changes in the architectural setting of the *Presentation*. Veronese's *Visitation* (Barber Institute of Fine Arts, Birmingham) appears to have inspired Rubens' *Visitation*.

PROV. Giovanelli coll., Venice, before 1732 until before 1933. Acquired from Dr. Vitale Bloch 1935.

EXH. Amsterdam, Goudstikker, 'Rubens', 1933 (2 and 3).

LIT. See *Catalogue* I and *Addenda*; also: *Catalogue* 1937, no.6; subsequently: F. Baudouin, *Rubens before 1620*, 1972, pp.59ff. (for history of commission; no ref. to Numbers 64–5); K. Renger in *Zeitschrift für Kunstgeschichte*, XXXVII, 1974, pp.16ff.; T. L. Glen, *Rubens and the Counter Reformation* (1975 thesis), 1977, pp.72, 242; J. S. Held, *The Oil Sketches of Peter Paul Rubens*, 1980, nos.357, 358.

Sir Peter Paul Rubens (1577–1640)

66 *The Family of Jan Brueghel the Elder*

Panel. 124·5×94·6
Inv. no.18

COLOUR PLATE XI

The sitters have been identified as the artist and friend of Rubens, Jan Brueghel the Elder (1568–1625), his second wife, Catharina van Marienbergh, and their eldest surviving children, Peter (b.1608) and Elisabeth (b.1609). The apparent ages of the children, who were both to die of cholera, like their father, in 1625, indicate a date of *c*.1612–13. The evidence of the composition, the different handling apparent in the figure of Jan Brueghel, and the existence of a copy lacking that figure, suggest that he is a later addition by the artist. Considerable alterations to Catharina's headdress are also visible. A number of other copies and versions record the present appearance of this portrait. Its early history (see below) and Rubens' authorship, which has been doubted, are now fully established by documentation. As Mr. Walter Melion pointed out, the bracelets worn by Catharina, one of which her son appears to be indicating, can be seen in a number of Jan Brueghel's still-life and allegorical paintings.

PROV. Jan Brueghel the Elder; Ambrosius Brueghel; Jan Borrekens; Anna Brueghel-Teniers; David Teniers III; by descent until early 18th cent.; Duchess of Cumberland in 1789; W. A. Coats by 1904, sold Christie's, 10 June 1927 (132); J. A. Coats, sold Christie's, 12 April 1935 (82); bought Sabin Galleries, London. Acquired London 1948.

EXH. R. B. A. Galleries, 1927 (Coats coll.) (288); Amsterdam, Rijksmuseum, 'International Art Trade', 1936 (136); R.A., 'Holbein and other Masters', 1950 (230).

LIT. See *Catalogue* I and *Addenda*; subsequently: K. Ertz, *Jan Brueghel der Ältere. Die Gemälde*, 1979, pp.442f.

67

Sir Peter Paul Rubens (1577–1640)

67 *The Death of Hippolytus*

Panel. 51×64·5
Inv. no.19

There exists no large finished picture based on this sketch, although a replica, drawings and another composition of the subject are known, or known to have existed. The present panel was overpainted with incidental detail in the late 18th or early 19th century, as shown in an engraving by Maria Cosway; this was removed in 1936. The figure of Hippolytus is derived from Michelangelo's drawing of Tityus (Royal coll., Windsor) and appears in a number of other guises in Rubens' work, from *The Death of Argus* (Cologne) of 1611 onwards. The present painting appears to be a year or two later than this. The rearing and plunging horses resemble those in the *Conversion of S. Paul* in this collection (Number 69). Hippolytus' death is caused by the appearance out of the sea of Poseidon's bull, in answer to the curse of Theseus who mistakenly believed his son to have dishonoured his own wife, Phaedra.

PROV. Sir Abraham Hume; 3rd Earl of Brownlow (died 1921), sold Christie's, 4 May 1923 (83); private coll., Berlin. Acquired Basle 1936.

EXH. British Institution, 1835 (86), and 1838 (65); R.A., 1893 (86); New Gallery, 1899/1900 (119).

LIT. See *Catalogue* 1 and *Addenda*; also: *Catalogue* 1937, no.7; subsequently: J. S. Held, *The Oil Sketches of Peter Paul Rubens*, 1980, no.245.

69

68

Sir Peter Paul Rubens (1577–1640)

68 *The Conversion of S. Paul*

Pancl. 56×79
Inv. no.20

For discussion see under Number 69.

PROV. Brussels art market, 1923; Franz Koenigs, Haarlem. Acquired 1940 from the Koenigs coll.

EXH. Amsterdam, Goudstikker, 'Rubens', 1933 (9); Rotterdam, Boymans Museum, 'Koenigs coll.', 1935 (20); Brussels, Musée Royal des Beaux-Arts, 'Esquisses de Rubens' 1937 (29).

LIT. See *Catalogue* I and *Addenda*; subsequently: J. S. Held, *The Oil Sketches of Peter Paul Rubens*, 1980, no.421.

Sir Peter Paul Rubens (1577–1640)

69 *The Conversion of S. Paul*

Panel. 95·2×120·7
Inv. no.21

Numbers 68 and 69 and Number 180 (a drawing, q.v.) demonstrate three stages of evolution in a composition dating probably from *c.*1613–16. The oil sketch (68), which is, for Rubens, unusually hard to read, is generally thought to precede the drawing (180) and the design appears then to have been expanded to encompass two finished companion paintings, Number 69 and *The Defeat of Sennacherib* (Munich). As in the *Conversion of S. Paul* painted in Italy *c.*1602 (formerly Antwerp, Rockox House), Rubens was inspired by 16th-cent. Italian representations of the subject. His admiration, also, of Elsheimer's *Conversion of S. Paul*

70

(Frankfurt) is apparent in the drawing (180), in Number 69 and its pendant in Munich, and also in the large *Conversion* (formerly Berlin, now destroyed) which has been dated *c*.1616–18 (preparatory oil sketch, Oxford, Ashmolean). From X-rays it appears that the present panel had previously been used, upside down, and that the finished painting underwent numerous changes. Held (1980, see LIT.) considers some parts, including the celestial figures, to belong to a 'reworking' of *c*.1620, the date to which he also assigns the *Conversion* formerly in Berlin, while the rest of Number 69, as well as the oil sketch (68) and drawing (180), he dates 1610–12.

PROV. (?) Prince of Orange, Het Loo, sale; Johann Wilhelm von der Pfalz, Düsseldorf; transferred to Munich 1806; Alte Pinakothek, Munich (transferred to Speyer Gallery by 1927); disposed of in exchange by Alte Pinakothek, 1938. Acquired Paris 1938.

LIT. See *Catalogue* I and *Addenda*; subsequently: J. Rowlands, *Rubens Drawings and Sketches*, British Museum, 1977, p.33; M. Jaffé, *Rubens and Italy*, 1977, pp.14, 53; J. S. Held, *The Oil Sketches of Peter Paul Rubens*, 1980, under nos.421, 422.

PLATE XI Sir Peter Paul Rubens *The Family of Jan Brueghel the Elder* cat.66

PLATE XII Sir Peter Paul Rubens *The Entombment* CAT.71

PLATE XIII Sir Peter Paul Rubens *Landscape by Moonlight* cat.89

PLATE XIV Sir Peter Paul Rubens *Esther before Ahasuerus* cat.75

Sir Peter Paul Rubens (1577–1640)

70 *The Daughters of Cecrops discovering Erichthonius*

Panel. 39·9×48·8
Inv. no.22

This is a sketch, though with marked differences, for the large painting in the Liechtenstein coll., generally dated *c.*1615–17. Erichthonius was accidentally conceived by Vulcan while attempting to ravish Minerva; Mother Earth (shown here as a fountain statue of Diana of Ephesus) gave birth to him in the form of a half-serpent, and Minerva entrusted him in a sealed basket to Herse, Aglauros, and Pandrosos, the daughters of King Cecrops of Attica. Rubens shows the moment when Aglauros disobeys Minerva's command and opens the basket (in alternative versions of the tale the child is normal but is found lying beside a serpent). Though some authors believed the story to have had a tragic consequence, the suicide of the horrified sisters, Rubens' treatment appears to reflect the happier version told by Ovid (*Metamorphoses*, II, 553–563). The obscure significance of the shadowy figure behind Herse has been much discussed. The subject, to which Rubens returned in the 1630s (fragment of painting in Oberlin, Ohio; sketch in Stockholm), appears to have been seen as a celebration of nature and fecundity.

PROV. Van Schorel, sold Antwerp, 7 June 1774 (21) (?); Sale, Tencé, Lille, 17 Sept. 1860 (92); bought Lille, 1897, by M. Nicolle. Acquired from Mme Nicolle, Paris, 1953.

LIT. See *Catalogue* I and *Addenda;* subsequently: K. Renger in *Zeitschrift für Kunstgeschichte*, XXXVII, 1974, pp.22f.; J. S. Held in *Zeitschrift für Kunstgeschichte*, XXXIX, 1976, pp.34ff.; J. S. Held, *The Oil Sketches of Peter Paul Rubens*, 1980, no.231.

Sir Peter Paul Rubens (1577–1640)

71 *The Entombment*

Panel. 83·3×61·2
Inv. no.23

COLOUR PLATE XII

Apparently a *modello*, of unusually large size, for an unknown and perhaps unexecuted large-scale painting. A number of copies of the present painting are known, including one by Carl Spitzweg. Rubens' source of inspiration was Caravaggio's *Entombment* (Vatican) of which he had painted a closer version (National Gallery of Canada, Ottawa), scarcely larger than Number 71, soon after his return from Italy. A drawing in Amsterdam (Rijksprentenkabinet) shows an intermediate stage between the Ottawa painting and the present one; these compositional changes, and the differences in colour and technique, indicate a date, more generally associated with the violently Baroque phase in Rubens' art, of *c.*1616–18.

PROV. Count Schönborn, Pommersfelden, by 1719; probably acquired from Schönborn coll. after mid-19th cent. by M. Haro; Haro sale, Paris, 3of. May 1892 (46); Baron Vitta, France. Acquired Paris 1953.

LIT. See *Catalogue* I and *Addenda;* subsequently: M. Jaffé, *Rubens and Italy*, 1977, p.58; J. S. Held, *The Oil Sketches of Peter Paul Rubens*, 1980, no.365.

71

Rubens and the Jesuit Church in Antwerp (Numbers 72–77)

Rubens' work for the church of S. Ignatius of Loyola (now S. Charles Borromeo), initiated perhaps in 1613 (see Number 72), included designs for the sculptural decoration of the building (begun 1615) and two great altarpieces (before 1620; Kunsthistorisches Museum, Vienna) and culminated in the decoration of the flat ceilings of the aisles, galleries and entrance bay of the church. In 1620 he contracted to provide thirty-nine *modelli* from which assistants (principally van Dyck) might paint the large (*c.*3×4 m.) canvases. These canvases, inspired by the great Venetians, principally Veronese, were finished in 1621 and fitted into wooden compartments – Venetian style – before consecration, 12 Sept. 1621. The subjects were New Testament scenes and their Old Testament prototypes in the galleries, alternately rectangular and octagonal, and single male and female saints in the aisles and west end, alternately octagonal and oval. The ceilings were destroyed by fire, 18 July 1718. Reconstruction of the cycle is based on written descriptions, and series of drawings made immediately before the tragedy: Jacob de Witt's series of 1711–12 (lost but recorded in his own copies, including a set of watercolours in this collection, and engraved by J. Punt) and C. B. Müller's drawings made six months before the fire (engraved in part by J. J. Preissler). Only a couple of drawings by Rubens for the project are known, a few preparatory *grisaille* sketches (including Number 73) and about twenty-five *modelli* (including Numbers 74–77); these, preserved by Rubens, were to be of use to him again when preparing his other great ceiling decoration, for the Banqueting House in Whitehall (see Number 84).

LIT. Detailed account by J. R. Martin in *Corpus Rubenianum*, I, *The Ceiling Paintings for the Jesuit Church in Antwerp*, 1968.

Sir Peter Paul Rubens (1577–1640)

72 *The Coronation of the Virgin*

Panel. 46×62
Inv. no.301
See introduction above

Possibly a very early idea for the Jesuit church ceiling. The octagonal format and the foreshortening, although moderate, suggest a connection with the project but the style indicates a date well before 1620. In 1613 the first plans for the church were submitted to Rome; Rubens' connection with the Antwerp Jesuits at that date is established and it is possible that he submitted then this first *modello* for the ceiling. In the event the canvas of this subject – at the west end of the south gallery – was rectangular, as was the *modello* of 1620 (Louvre); there is also a preliminary *grisaille* (Rotterdam). Strangely, the subject is not listed in the contract. The present composition appears, enlarged, in versions of Teniers' *Gallery of David Teniers*. Held (1980, see LIT.) considers Number 72 to be unconnected with the Jesuit church commission and to be a *modello* of *c.*1617, perhaps for the larger picture recorded by Teniers.

PROV. H. M. Gutmann, sold Berlin, 12ff. Apr. 1934 (43); R. von Schnitzler, Cologne; Freiherr C. von Schröder, Hamburg; Stanley Loomis, sold Sotheby, 2 July 1958 (134). Acquired at sale.

72

EXH. Cologne, Kunstverein, 1934; Brussels, Musée Royal des Beaux-Arts, 'Esquisses de Rubens', 1937 (36); Helsinki, 'Rubens', 1952–3 (VIII); Brussels, 'Rubens', 1953 (7).

LIT. See *Catalogue* IV and *Addenda*; subsequently: J. S. Held, *The Oil Sketches of Peter Paul Rubens*, 1980, no.380.

Sir Peter Paul Rubens (1577–1640)

73 *David slaying Goliath*

Panel. 25·5×19
Inv. no.25
See introduction on p.50

This is unusual among the *grisaille* sketches for the Jesuit church in that it shows Rubens' first idea for the principal figures only of the composition and in containing indications of colour. The figure of David appears to derive from Titian's *Cain* (S. Maria della Salute, Venice), which, with its two companion paintings, then all in S. Spirito, was one of the chief inspirations for Rubens' ceiling paintings. The presumed *modello* for this subject is lost. The ceiling painting was rectangular and in the north gallery of the church (no.21 in the contract); etched by Paneels, 1630.

PROV. ?Maximilien de Hase, sold Brussels, 10 June 1782 (5); ?Comte de Cuypers, sold Brussels, 27 Apr. 1802 (114); C. Spruyt, sold Ghent, 28ff July 1806 (167), bought Maes; Waltner, Paris; Dubaut, Paris. Acquired Paris 1937.

EXH. Brussels, Musée Royal des Beaux-Arts, 'Esquisses de Rubens', 1937 (65).

LIT. See *Catalogue* I and *Addenda*; subsequently: J. Foucart in *Revue du Louvre*, XXIV, 1, 1974, pp.22f.; J. S. Held, *The Oil Sketches of Peter Paul Rubens*, 1980, no.11.

73

51

74

Sir Peter Paul Rubens (1577–1640)

74 *Solomon receiving the Queen of Sheba*

Panel. 40·5×46·1
Inv. no.26
See introduction on p.50

This panel was, from before 1767 until 1945, enlarged at top and bottom to match Number 75; the two *modelli* shared, as pendants, the same history. They are, in effect, mirror images of each other, each indebted to Veronese's *Esther before Ahasuerus* (S. Sebastiano, Venice). Rubens was clearly still experimenting with the shapes of the scenes: the octagon was enlarged at the corners during execution, and the eventual ceiling painting, in the north gallery, was to be a rectangle (no.23 in the contract).

PROV. (for Numbers 74 and 75): J. de Julienne, sold Paris, 30 Mar. ff. 1767 (100), bought Donjeux; Le Doux, sold Paris, 24 Apr. 1775 (21); Dubois, sold Paris, 20 Dec. 1785 (10); C.–A. de Calonne, sold London, 23 Mar. 1795 (61); Sale (Bryan), London, 27 Apr. 1795 (99); M. Bryan, sold London, 17ff. May 1798 (17); W. Y. Ottley, sold London, 25 May 1811 (70, 71); J. Webb, sold London, 30f. May 1821 (139, 140); Norton, sold London, 22 Oct. 1830; Sale, London, 28f. Apr. 1837 (26, 27); Sir Francis Cook. Acquired from the Cook coll. 1945.

EXH. (for Numbers 74 and 75): Dowdeswell Galleries, 1912; Burlington Fine Arts Club, 1923–4 (19); R.A., 'Flemish and Belgian Art', 1927 (324, 325); Antwerp, 1930 (249, 250).

LIT. See *Catalogue* 1 and *Addenda*; also: W. Buchanan, *Memoirs of Painting*, 1824, 1, pp.238, 287; subsequently: J. S. Held, *The Oil Sketches of Peter Paul Rubens*, 1980, no.12.

75

Sir Peter Paul Rubens (1577–1640)

75 *Esther before Ahasuerus*

Panel. 48·8×47

COLOUR PLATE XIV

Inv. no.27

See introduction on p.50

This *modello* replaced an earlier one (Akademie, Vienna) which was a twelve-sided composition with larger figures; in the final ceiling painting, in the south gallery (no.27 in the contract), Rubens retained the octagonal shape of the present picture, but substituted an open sky for the dome. A number of Venetian sources can be traced, the principal inspiration being Veronese (see under Number 74). Rubens used this *modello* again, ten years later, for the *Union of England and Scotland* on the ceiling of the Banqueting House in Whitehall. For the subject see under Number 117.

PROV. See Number 74.

EXH. See Number 74.

LIT. See Number 74 (J. S. Held, op. cit., no.14, and pp.205, 208f.).

76

Sir Peter Paul Rubens (1577–1640)

76 *The Temptation of Christ*

Panel. 34×32
Inv. no.28
See introduction on p.50

Rubens followed this *modello* closely and retained its octagonal shape for the canvas in the north gallery of the church. The subject is not listed in the contract. It was this *modello*, not the ceiling painting, which Christoffel Jegher followed, with certain adjustments, in his woodcut of 1633.

PROV. ?Comte de Cuypers, Ghent; ?L. J. Cocquereau, sold Brussels, 25ff. Aug. 1806 (89), bought Vervier; Schamp d'Averschoot, sold Ghent, 14 Sept. ff. 1840 (136); A. Ysabie, Ghent. Acquired Paris 1938.

EXH. Brussels, Musée des Beaux-Arts, 'Esquisses de Rubens', 1937 (69a).

LIT. See *Catalogue* I and *Addenda*; subsequently: J. Foucart in *Revue du Louvre*, XXIV, 1, 1974, p.24; J. Rowlands, *Rubens Drawings and Sketches*, British Museum, 1977, p.107; J. S. Held, *The Oil Sketches of Peter Paul Rubens*, 1980, no.19.

Sir Peter Paul Rubens (1577–1640)

77 *S. Gregory the Great* (fragment)

Panel. 43·5×33
Inv. no.29
See introduction on p.50

The top and left parts of the *modello* (estimated original size *c.*50×60 cm.) are missing; subsequent additions in these areas were removed after 1933. Before mutilation the *modello* would have shown S. Gregory adoring the Virgin and Child who were raised on clouds. The finished canvas, in the westernmost bay of the south aisle, was octagonal (no.26 in the contract).

PROV. Acquired in Italy by Paul Mila (1798–1866), Berlin; Steinrück coll., Berlin; L. Rosenheim, Düsseldorf, sold Amsterdam, 9 Dec. 1930 (21). Acquired Amsterdam 1933.

EXH. Düsseldorf, 'Alte Meister in Privatbesitz', 1921 (69); Berlin, 'Alte Meister aus Berliner Besitz', 1925 (331); Siegen, Museum, 1927; Amsterdam, Goudstikker, 'Rubens', 1933 (13).

LIT. See *Catalogue* I and *Addenda*; also: *Catalogue* 1937, no.8; subsequently: J. S. Held, *The Oil Sketches of Peter Paul Rubens*, 1980, no.35.

77

78

Sir Peter Paul Rubens (1577–1640)

78 *Sacrifice in a Temple (after Elsheimer)*

Canvas on panel. 47·8×60·8
Inv. no.30

An adaptation of Elsheimer's *Il Contento* (National Gallery of Scotland), which Rubens could have seen in Rome and again, possibly, in the Netherlands in *c.*1620–30, the decade to which this painting appears to belong – although, as the colour differences indicate, it could have been based on a drawing. Rubens used only the left half of Elsheimer's composition, and transformed it into the interior of a temple, exploiting the effects of artificial light, and translating, with numerous changes, the obscure subject of *Il Contento* into a sacrifice to Venus and Mars, with a background tapestry which can be identified as the Judgement of Paris – in hommage to Venus.

PROV. Inventory after Rubens' death (119); Jeremias Wildens (died 1653; inv. no.643); General Sir Francis Davies; Miss Grizel Davies, sold Sotheby, 21 June 1950 (106d). Acquired London 1950.

LIT. See *Catalogue* 1 and *Addenda*; subsequently: K. Andrews, *Adam Elsheimer. Il Contento*, 1971, p.20; M. Jaffé, *Rubens and Italy*, 1977, p.54.

79

Sir Peter Paul Rubens (1577–1640)

79 *Modello for a Title Page*

Paper on canvas. 31×21·4
Inv. no.33

This *grisaille* was engraved (not in reverse) by Cornelius Galle for Balthasar Corderius' commentary on S. Luke's Gospel, *Catena sexaginta quinque Graecorum patrum in S. Lucam*, Plantin, Antwerp, 1628. The skin of S. Luke's symbol, the bull, was designed to carry the title; the evangelist, above, is flanked by the symbols of the three other evangelists and by Truth, who places about his neck the *catena* (chain) of the title. SS. Augustine and Gregory of Nazianzus flank the coat-of-arms to be engraved below, that of the Emperor Ferdinand II, to whom the book was dedicated. Rubens, who was paid 20 florins for the work, rejected the author's complaint that the figure of Truth was insufficiently covered.

PROV. G. Uilenbroek, sold Amsterdam, 23 Oct. 1741 (3); H. Tersmitten, sold Amsterdam, 23 Sept. 1754 (436); W. Y. Ottley, sold London 6ff. July 1807 (517); J. Smith, London, 1830; Mrs F. M. Noel, sold Sotheby, 29 Nov. 1944 (93). Acquired from Christopher Norris 1946.

LIT. See *Catalogue 1* and *Addenda*; subsequently: *Corpus Rubenianum*, XXI, J. R. Judson and C. van de Velde, *Book Illustrations and Title-Pages*, 1978, I, pp.252f., cat.58a, and *passim*; J. S. Held, *The Oil Sketches of Peter Paul Rubens*, 1980, no.303.

Sir Peter Paul Rubens (1577–1640)

80 *Baldassare Castiglione (after Raphael)*

Panel. 89·5×67·5
Brand of Antwerp guild on back of panel
Inv. no.24

A copy of Raphael's celebrated portrait in the Louvre. Rubens' extension of the composition to show the hands entirely, together with the similar interpretation in a drawing by Rembrandt (1639; Albertina) has sometimes been taken as proof that Raphael's original has since been cut down. There is convincing evidence, however, that Raphael's masterpiece is unaltered and that both Rembrandt and Rubens preferred a format to suit the style of their time, as in Rubens' copy of Holbein's *Sir Thomas More* (Prado) of about the same date (*c.*1630). In both cases it appears that Rubens' versions must have been made from copies of the originals. He could have seen Raphael's portrait in Mantua about a quarter of a century earlier than the date indicated by the style of his copy; to have painted from the original at this later period Rubens would have had to visit the newly-arrived collection of van Uffelen in Amsterdam, soon after 1630; no such visit is recorded.

PROV. Inventory after Rubens' death, no.78. Acquired Amsterdam 1936.

LIT. See *Catalogue 1* and *Addenda*; also: *Catalogue 1937*, no.9; subsequently: W. Stechow in *Rubens before 1620*, 1972, p.23; M. Jaffé, *Rubens in Italy*, 1977, pp.15, 27; J. Shearman in *Revue du Louvre et des Musées de France*, 1979, XXIX, 4, pp.262ff.

80

81

Scenes from the Life of Achilles (for Numbers 81 and 82)

Nothing is known about this commission for a series of eight tapestry designs, but Rubens probably made them for his father-in-law, the tapestry merchant, Daniel Fourment, in the early 1630s. Since classical times the life of Achilles had apparently never been illustrated as a whole cycle, and Rubens' sources were literary – both classical and modern. Subjects chosen were: Achilles dipped in the River Styx, Achilles instructed by Chiron, Achilles discovered among the Daughters of Lycomedes, Thetis receiving Arms for Achilles from Hephaestus, the Wrath of Achilles, Briseis restored to Achilles, Achilles vanquishing Hector, and the Death of Achilles. The tapestries, of which few, and no complete sets, survive, were each *c*.4 m. high and *c*.35 m. in total width; Delacroix in his *Journal* has left a description of a complete set. All the *modelli* survive: in Sarasota (1), Prado (3), Pau Museum (2) and Numbers 81 and 82; and all the preparatory sketches: Boymans Museum, Rotterdam (7, including those for Numbers 81 and 82) and Detroit (1). The cartoons are lost.

Sir Peter Paul Rubens (1577–1640)

81 *The Wrath of Achilles*

Panel. 106×108
Inv. no.31
See introduction above

Rubens follows closely Homer's account of this episode (*Iliad*, 1, 193–200). Agamemnon, having threatened to take Briseis from Achilles, sits enthroned before the enraged hero; Achilles is restrained from drawing his sword by Athene, whom he alone can see, on the left are Diomedes and the aged Nestor. The simulated sculpture personifies Discord (left) and Blind Fury, and the chained lion represents Achilles' strength restrained by Athene. There is some disagreement about the involvement of assistants in Numbers 81 and 82, but almost the entire visible surface, at least, is generally agreed to be autograph (although not by Held, 1980, see LIT.).

PROV. ?Daniel Fourment, ?Peter Fourment, Antwerp; ?Gerard van der Strecken and others, Brussels – until late 17th cent.; Dukes of Infantado, Madrid, until 1841; Duke of Osuña, Madrid; Marques of Salamanca, 1st sale, Paris, 3ff. June 1867 (105), 2nd sale, Paris, 25f. Jan. 1875 (67); Dreyfus sale, G. Petit, Paris, 29 May 1889 (109); Vicomte de Lyrot, Paris. Acquired Paris 1937.

LIT. See *Catalogue* 1 and *Addenda*; subsequently: *Corpus Rubenianum*, X, E. Haverkamp Begemann, *The Achilles Series*, 1975, cat.5b, pp.52–66, 121f.; J. S. Held, *The Oil Sketches of Peter Paul Rubens*, 1980, under no.123.

Sir Peter Paul Rubens (1577–1640)

82 *The Death of Achilles*

Panel. 107×108   COLOUR PLATE XV
Inv. no.32
See introduction above

Homer gives no account, beyond predictions, of Achilles' death, and Rubens' source was either the 4th cent. Servius Grammaticus or a modern text. Achilles,

82

about to marry Polyxena in the temple of Apollo, is dying from the arrow shot through his sole (at that time considered the vulnerable spot, rather than his heel) by Paris, avenging the death of his brothers, Hector and Troilus, and guided by Apollo, champion of the Trojans. Achilles is supported by (?)Ulysses. The simulated sculpture represents Aphrodite with Cupid (left) and Apollo, and the fox killing the eagle, below, symbolizes the cunning which destroyed the hero.

PROV. As for Number 81.

LIT. See *Catalogue* I and *Addenda*; subsequently: *Corpus Rubenianum*, X, E. Haverkamp Begemann, *The Achilles Series*, 1975, cat.8b, pp.57–66, 140f.; J. S. Held, *The Oil Sketches of Peter Paul Rubens*, 1980, under no.128.

Sir Peter Paul Rubens (1577–1640)

83 *A Landscape*

Panel. 49·2×64·8
Inv. no.35

This landscape, formerly overpainted, has the appearance of being an unfinished painting, rather than a sketch; in the middle ground and distance are areas much more highly finished than the foreground and sky. It has been dated *c.*1630, but a resemblance to the right-hand side of the *Rainbow Landscape* (Wallace Coll., London) suggests a possible later dating in the mid 1630s.

PROV. Mr. de Pesters, sold Prestage, 2 Apr. 1756 (33), bought Sir William Lowther; Earl of Dartmouth. Acquired from Mrs Otto Gutekunst 1939.

EXH. Leeds, 1868 (826); Brussels, 'L'Art Belge au XVIIᵉ siècle', 1910 (403); Ipswich, 'Gainsborough', 1927 (1); Burlington Fine Arts Club, 1936/7 (34).

LIT. See *Catalogue* I.

83

84

85

Sir Peter Paul Rubens (1577–1640)

84 *The Bounty of James I triumphing over Avarice*

Panel. 54×31
Inv. no.36

This *modello* is for one of the four oval canvases, representing the virtues of James I, in the corners of the Banqueting House ceiling. First broached in 1621, the ceiling was probably commissioned when Rubens was in England, 1629–30. The first oil sketch for the whole ceiling, of about that time (Mrs. H. Brand, Glynde), shows the first idea for *Bounty* (or *Liberality*). Other detailed *modelli* like Number 84 survive, perhaps submitted to Charles I, then used by Rubens and assistants in Antwerp, where the nine huge canvases were painted by 1634, reaching England in 1635. Rubens' sources were principally Venetian, as was the structure of Inigo Jones' ceiling, but the figure of Bounty derives from one of Michelangelo's *Ignudi*; Rubens' copy made in the Sistine Chapel survives, as does the counterproof copy of the early 1630s (both British Museum), made perhaps with the figure of Bounty in mind.

PROV. Sir Joshua Reynolds, sold London, 14 May 1795 (37); Morgan coll., Breadalbane, sold Christie's, 27 Mar. 1925 (139); H. M. Clark, London; Franz Koenigs, Haarlem. Acquired 1940 from the Koenigs coll.

EXH. Amsterdam, Goudstikker, 'Rubens', 1933 (42); Rotterdam, Boymans Museum, 'Koenigs coll.', 1935 (35); Brussels, Musée Royal des Beaux-Arts, 'Esquisses de Rubens', 1937 (99); Tate Gallery, 'Age of Charles I', 1972–3 (40).

LIT. See *Catalogue* 1 and *Addenda*; subsequently: J. Rowlands, *Rubens Drawings and Sketches*, British Museum, 1977, p.45; J. S. Held, *The Oil Sketches of Peter Paul Rubens*, 1980, no.143.

Sir Peter Paul Rubens (1577–1640)

85 *Jan van Montfort*

Canvas. 107×90
Inv. no.37

The sitter's identification is based on his resemblance to van Dyck's portrait of Jan van (or Jean de) Montfort, 1627–8 (Kunsthistorisches Museum, Vienna), in which the same badges of office are also worn. X-rays of the present portrait reveal an earlier version beneath, the sitter wearing a lace collar. Montfort (fl. 1596–1649), a friend of Rubens, was a medallist and, from 1613, Master General of the Mint at the Brussels court of Archduchess Isabella. The portrait has been dated, on stylistic grounds, *c.*1635.

PROV. Sir Thomas Sebright, Beechwood. Acquired from Sir Giles Sebright 1936.

LIT. See *Catalogue* 1 and *Addenda*; also: *Catalogue* 1937, no.10.

86

Sir Peter Paul Rubens (1577–1640)

86 *The Assumption of the Virgin*

Panel. 49×36·5
Inv. no.38

A *modello* for the large altarpiece (5 m. high) in the Liechtenstein collection (Vaduz), painted apparently for the Carthusian church, Brussels, *c.*1635. Another *modello* (Yale) appears to be closer in composition to the altarpiece, although less finished and colourful; a drawing after Number 86 is in the Museum Boymans-van Beuningen, Rotterdam. This seems to be the last appearance in his work of a subject in demand almost throughout Rubens' career. Traces of another composition, top right corner, indicate that the panel had been used for the beginnings of an earlier design, probably upside down.

PROV. The Marquess of Headfort, Headfort House, Ireland. Acquired London 1937.

LIT. See *Addenda*; subsequently: *Corpus Rubenianum*, XXI, J. R. Judson and C. van de Velde, *Book Illustrations and Title-Pages*, 1978, I, p.145 n.; J. S. Held, *The Oil Sketches of Peter Paul Rubens*, 1980, no.378.

87

Sir Peter Paul Rubens (1577–1640)

87 *Hercules or Atlas bearing the Heavens*

Panel. 25×16·5
Inv. no.39

This and the following item belong among over fifty surviving sketches for the decoration of the Torre de la Parada, Philip IV's hunting lodge outside Madrid, commissioned 1636 and completed 1638. This immense ensemble, now difficult to reconstruct, included more than one hundred works by Rubens and his circle, of which over sixty were Ovidian mythologies, and fifty were animal and hunting scenes. Of Rubens' large-scale paintings fourteen survive; thirty-eight of the original paintings from the Torre are in the Prado – many of poor workshop quality, contrasting with the brilliance of Rubens' preparatory sketches. The finished canvas of Number 87 is lost, but a copy after the sketch is in the Prado. There is conflicting evidence for the identification of the figure: inventories and iconography indicate Atlas, but Hercules is suggested by a related sheet of studies of his Labours (British Museum); there is also a transcription of a lost related drawing by Rubens in the 'MS Johnson' belonging to the Princes Gate collection.

PROV. II. Oppenheimer, sold Christie's, 24 July 1936 (16). Acquired London 1937.

EXH. R.A., 'Flemish and Belgian Art', 1927 (332a); Brussels, Musée Royal des Beaux-Arts, 'Esquisses de Rubens', 1937 (105).

LIT. See *Catalogue* 1 and *Addenda*; subsequently: *Corpus Rubenianum*, IX, S. Alpers, *The Decoration of the Torre de la Parada*, 1971, pp.182f., cat.5a, and *passim*.; J. S. Held, *The Oil Sketches of Peter Paul Rubens*, 1980, no.172.

Sir Peter Paul Rubens (1577–1640)

88 *Hercules killing the Hydra*

Panel. 22·5×10·5
Inscribed upper right, '9'
Inv. no.40

For the commission see Number 87. The finished painting after this sketch is lost; a copy by Mazo is in the Prado; a drawing after the lost painting, in the present collection (inv. no.325), may be by Rubens, made in preparation for a woodcut.

PROV. Mrs. Lorna Mary de Satgé, sold Christie's, 23 June 1933 (99). Acquired at sale.

LIT. See *Addenda*; also: *Catalogue* 1937, no.11; subsequently: *Corpus Rubenianum*, IX, S. Alpers, *The Decoration of the Torre de la Parada*, 1971, p.220, cat.30a, and *passim*; J. S. Held, *The Oil Sketches of Peter Paul Rubens*, 1980, no.192.

88

89

Sir Peter Paul Rubens (1577–1640)

89 *Landscape by Moonlight*

Panel. 63×89   COLOUR PLATE XIII
Inv. no.41

The creation of this celebrated landscape from Rubens' last years can be traced through X-rays and the shapes of the panels: wide additions to the top and right were made during the course of execution and figures in the centre foreground – indistinct but presumed to be for a *Rest on the Flight into Egypt* – were later painted out. There is an engraving by Bolswert, and an engraving (anon.), not reversed, with an added *Flight into Egypt*. Since at least the 18th century this landscape has been in England. Reynolds used it, when in his collection, as an object lesson in colour and light in his *Eighth Discourse* (1778); its influence at that time can be seen in Gainsborough's work. Constable saw the picture at Samuel Rogers' house in 1836, and observed 'He was pleased with my pointing out the falling or shooting star in his exquisite Rubens'; and on his death-bed it is recorded that Constable's 'feet nearly touched a print of the beautiful moonlight by Rubens, belonging to Mr Rogers.'

PROV. Possibly no.173 in inventory after Rubens' death; James Boswell(?); Sir Joshua Reynolds by 1778, sold Christie's, 11ff. Mar. 1795 (85); Earl of Bessborough, sold Christie's, 5ff. Feb. 1801 (72); J. Willett Willett, sold London, 31ff May 1813 (84); Earl of Mulgrave, sold Christie's, 12 May 1832 (70); Samuel Rogers, sold Christie's, 28 Apr. ff. 1856 (593), bought Lord Wardle; Earl of Dudley, sold Christie's, 25 June 1892 (30); Ludwig Mond; by descent. Acquired 1935 from Lord Melchett.

EXH. British Institution, 1815 (19); R.A., 1871 (350); New Gallery, 1897/8 (83) and 1899/1900 (137); R.A., 'Flemish and Belgian Art', 1927 (322); Spink and Sons, 1930 (19); R.A., 'Flemish Art', 1953/4 (183).

LIT. See *Catalogue* 1 and *Addenda*; also: C. R. Leslie, *Autobiographical Recollections*, 1860, I, p.158; *Catalogue* 1937, no.12; W. Stechow, *Dutch Landscape Painting*, 1966, pp.179f.; subsequently: J. Hayes, *Gainsborough*, 1975, p.222; M. Jaffé, *Rubens and Italy*, 1977, p.53.

Spanish School, Early Sixteenth Century: see Appendix I, inv. no.255

Hendrik van Steenwyck the Younger (1580–1649)

90 *S. Jerome in his Study*

Panel. 27·4×21·7
Signed and dated, lower left, 'H. V. STEINWICK 1624'
Inv. no.176

Based closely on an engraving by Theodor de Bry (1528–1598) which bears Dürer's monogram, but is actually after a drawing ascribed to Ludwig Krug (*c*.1488/90–1532; Vienna, Albertina). Hendrik van Steenwyck the Younger, who occasionally collaborated with Jan Brueghel the Elder, was born in Antwerp, of Dutch origin, and spent much of his life in London, where he died. He was much admired by Charles I and fellow collectors.

PROV. Sale, Sotheby, 30 June 1948 (87). Acquired at sale.

LIT. See *Addenda*.

90

PLATE XV Sir Peter Paul Rubens *The Death of Achilles* cat.82

PLATE XVI Giovanni Battista Tiepolo *The Immaculate Conception* cat. 112

Copies by David Teniers the Younger after the Italian Paintings in the Collection of Archduke Leopold Wilhelm of Austria (Numbers 91–104)

The fourteen small copies by David Teniers the Younger in this collection were painted after works in the collection of Archduke Leopold Wilhelm, during his Governorship of the Netherlands, 1647–56, when the chief part of the collection was acquired. Teniers was commissioned to paint these copies for engravers to make a series of prints, published – the first of many editions – in Brussels, 1660, as *Davidis Teniers Antverpiensis pictoris et a cvbicvlis Ser.^{mis} Principibvs Leopoldo Gvil. Archidvci & Joanni Avstriaco Theatrvm Pictorivm*; this, known as the *Theatrum Pictorium*, is one of the earliest published catalogues of paintings. The 245 engravings represent only part of the collection; Teniers' series of copies was incomplete when the Archduke left Brussels in May 1656; part of the collection was left behind for Teniers to complete the copies of Italian paintings (October 1656). The pictures were engraved again for Stampart and Brenner's 1735 *Prodromus . . .* of the Imperial collection in Vienna. Teniers' copies are widely dispersed, but 120 were in the Duke of Marlborough sale in 1886, including eleven of the following.

91

David Teniers the Younger (1610–1690)

91 *S. George or S. Liberalis and S. Rosalia or S. Cecilia (after Antonello da Messina)*

Panel. 24·5×18·5
Inv. no.48
See introduction above

Copy after a fragment, now lost, of Antonello da Messina's *San Cassiano Altarpiece*, of which three surviving fragments are in the Kunsthistorisches Museum, Vienna. Number 91 is engraved in the *Theatrum Pictorium* by I. Popels as after Bellini (no.6).

PROV. Earl of Wicklow, Shelton Abbey, sold 16 Oct. ff. 1950 (1589). Acquired London 1951.

David Teniers the Younger (1610–1690)

92 *Parable of the Wicked Husbandmen (after Domenico Fetti)*

Panel. 19·5×25·4
Inv. no.49
See introduction above

Copy after a painting by Domenico Fetti of which a version was formerly in the Kaiser Friedrich Museum, Berlin (now destroyed), and another is in the Currier Gallery, New Hampshire; it is engraved in the *Theatrum Pictorium* by Quirin Boel (no.214).

PROV. Acquired London 1951.

LIT. See *Addenda;* subsequently: P. Askew in *Currier Gallery of Art Bulletin*, III, 1973, pp.10ff.

92

93

David Teniers the Younger (1610–1690)

93 *Ecce Homo (after Alessandro Varotari?)*

Panel. 23×17
Inv. no.304
See introduction on p.65

Copy after a lost painting, apparently by Alessandro Varotari (il Padovanino). It is not recorded in the Archduke's 1659 inventory, but appears engraved in the *Prodromus* of 1735. It is engraved in the *Theatrum Pictorium* by J. Troyen as after Varotari (no.238).

PROV. Marlborough sale, Christie's, 24 July ff. 1886 (189), bought Harle; Sale, Christie's, 26 Feb. 1960 (136). Acquired London 1960.

David Teniers the Younger (1610–1690)

94 *S. Sebastian (after Mantegna)*

Panel. 22·9×16·7
Inv. no.305
See introduction on p.65

Copy after Mantegna's painting in the Kunsthistorisches Museum, Vienna; the small horse and rider in the clouds has not been copied. It was engraved by J. Troyen in the *Theatrum Pictorium* as after 'A. Montani' (no.28).

PROV. Marlborough sale, Christie's, 24 July ff.1886 (87), bought Grindlay. Acquired London 1960.

94

95

David Teniers the Younger (1610–1690)

95 *Aeneas and Anchises with Ascanius (after Andrea Schiavone)*

Panel. 22·9×16·8
Inv. no.306
See introduction on p.65

Copy after a lost picture by Andrea Schiavone; it appears to be shown in one of Teniers' series of paintings of the Archduke's picture gallery in Brussels (Schleissheim). A picture corresponding except in its oblong format is listed in the archducal inventory of 1659; and a similar oblong picture was formerly in the Landesbildergalerie, Graz. Either there were two versions, or Teniers made arbitrary changes in his copy. Number 95 was engraved by C. Lauwers as after A. Schiavone in the *Theatrum Pictorium* (no.131).

PROV. Marlborough sale, Christie's, 24 July ff. 1886 (139). Acquired London 1960.

David Teniers the Younger (1610–1690)

96 *Portrait of a Man (after Titian)*

Panel. 22·4×17
Signed lower left 'DT' (?)
Inv. no.307
See introduction on p.65

Copy after Titian's portrait, formerly called *Filippo Strozzi*, in the Kunsthistorisches Museum, Vienna. The portrait was attributed to Tintoretto in the inventory of 1659; it was engraved as after Titian by L. Vorsterman the Younger in the *Theatrum Pictorium* (no.95).

PROV. Private coll., Paris, 1937. Acquired London 1960.

EXH. Basle, Kunsthalle, 'Künstlerkopien', 1937 (2).

96

97

David Teniers the Younger (1610–1690)

97 *Adam and Eve after the Expulsion (after Veronese)*

Panel. 22·7×31·1
Inv. no.308
See introduction on p.65

A copy, unusually large for the series, after Veronese's painting in the Kunsthistorisches Museum, Vienna. It was engraved by J. Troyen in the *Theatrum Pictorium* (no.118).

PROV. Marlborough sale, Christie's, 24 July ff. 1886 (132), bought Talbot; Private coll., London. Acquired London 1961.

David Teniers the Younger (1610–1690)

98 *Portrait of the Doge Nicolas da Ponte (after Tintoretto)*

Canvas laid down on panel. 16·8×12
Inv. no.309
See introduction on p.65

Copy after the portrait in the Kunsthistorisches Museum, Vienna, by Jacopo Tintoretto or his workshop. It was engraved by L. Vorsterman the Younger in the *Theatrum Pictorium* as by J. Tintoretto (no.97).

PROV. Marlborough sale, Christie's, 24 July ff. 1886 (122), bought Buxton; The Hon. Mrs. Frances Buxton, sold anon. Christie's, 8 June 1914 (96); Sir Hugh Lane; J. G. Hughes; Sale, Christie's, 17 July 1964 (93). Acquired at sale.

98

100

David Teniers the Younger (1610–1690)

99 *Portrait of a Venetian Senator (after Tintoretto)*

Canvas laid down on panel. 16·6×12
Inv. no.310
See introduction on p.65

Copy after Jacopo Tintoretto's portrait in the Kunsthistorisches Museum, Vienna. It was engraved by L. Vorsterman the Younger in the *Theatrum Pictorium* (no.103).

PROV. Marlborough sale, Christie's, 24 July ff., 1886 (125), bought Buxton; The Hon. Mrs. Frances Buxton, sold anon. Christie's, 8 June 1914 (96); Sir Hugh Lane; J. G. Hughes; Sale, Christie's, 17 July 1964 (93). Acquired at sale.

David Teniers the Younger (1610–1690)

100 *Susannah and the Elders (after Guido Reni)*

Panel. 17×22·5
Inv. no.311
See introduction on p.65

Copy after a lost painting by Guido Reni. As with Number 93, it is not recorded in the Archduke's inventory of 1659, but appears engraved in the *Prodromus* of 1735. The lost painting was probably the once celebrated original of a number of versions in other collections (e.g. London, National Gallery; Florence, Uffizi). It was engraved by P. Lisebetius in the *Theatrum Pictorium* as after 'I. Retto' – in error for 'Reno' (no.233).

99

102

PROV. Marlborough sale, Christie's, 24 July ff. 1886 (186), bought Murray; Johann Stumpf, sold Lepke, Berlin, 7 May 1918 (15). Acquired London 1966.

LIT. See *Catalogue* IV.

101

David Teniers the Younger (1610–1690)

101 *Cupid overcoming Pan (after Carracci)*

Panel. 22·2×16·8
Inv. no.312
See introduction on p.65

Copy after a lost painting described as by Carracci in the 1659 archducal inventory and in the *Prodromus* of 1735, as well as on J. Troyen's engraving in the *Theatrum Pictorium* (no.41). The subject is known in the work of Agostino and Annibale Carracci, and the attribution of the lost painting to one of the Carracci is probably correct. There is a closely related drawing in the Ashmolean, Oxford, now ascribed to Watteau; a version of Number 101 from the collection of the Princess Royal was recently on loan to Kenwood. The subject signifies the victory of divine over carnal love.

PROV. Lady Hampden, sold Christie's, 18 April 1834 (79), bought Norton; Charles Brind, sold Christie's, 12 May 1849 (40), bought Capron; Marlborough sale, Christie's, 24 July ff. 1886 (93), bought Agnew. Acquired Paris 1965.

EXH. British Institution, June 1848 (127).

LIT. See *Catalogue* IV.

David Teniers the Younger (1610–1690)

102 *The Good Samaritan (after Francesco Bassano)*

Panel. 17·5×23·4
Inv. no.313
See introduction on p.65

Copy after Francesco Bassano's painting in the Kunsthistorisches Museum, Vienna, which has been cut down on all four sides. It was engraved by Quirin Boel in the *Theatrum Pictorium* (no.152). There is a version of Number 102 (Metropolitan Museum of Art, New York) which has also been claimed as the original, and from the Marlborough sale.

PROV. Marlborough sale, Christie's, 24 July ff. 1886 (149), bought Buck. Acquired London 1967.

David Teniers the Younger (1610–1690)

103 *Portrait of a Sculptor (after G. B. Moroni)*

Paper on panel(?) 16·5×11·5
Inv. no.391
See introduction on p.65

Copy after Giovanni Battista Moroni's portrait in the Kunsthistorisches Museum, Vienna. It was engraved by L. Vorsterman the Younger in the *Theatrum Pictorium* as after Titian (no.59).

PROV. Marlborough sale, Christie's, 24 July ff. 1886 (104); Henri Leroux, Paris, sold Drouot, Paris, 30 Oct. 1968 (122). Acquired at sale.

LIT. See *Catalogue* VI.

103

104

David Teniers the Younger (1610–1690)

104 *S. Mary Magdalene in Ecstasy (after Palma Giovane?)*

Panel. 23·3×17·4
Inv. no.392
See introduction on p.65

Copy after a lost painting apparently by Palma Giovane; it was listed as on marble, by an unknown artist, in the 1659 archducal inventory, and appears in the *Prodromus* of 1735; in other inventories it appears as by Palma Giovane, as it does on T. van Kessel's engraving in the *Theatrum Pictorium* (no.171).

PROV. Marlborough sale, Christie's, 24 July ff. 1886 (151); Henri Leroux, Versailles; Sale, Dorotheum, Vienna, 22 Sept. 1970 (122). Acquired at sale.

David Teniers the Younger: see also Frans Franken the Younger and David Teniers the Younger

105

Giovanni Battista Tiepolo (1696–1770)

105 *Allegory of the Power of Eloquence*

Canvas. 46·5×67·5; within shaped border
Inv. no.340

Modello for the ceiling of the *salone* in the Palazzo Sandi, Venice, Tiepolo's first large fresco in a private palace, painted *c.* 1725 and still *in situ* (6·5×10·7 m.). The theme is illustrated by four mythologies, presided over by Minerva and Mercury in the centre (in the *modello*, clockwise from below): *Amphion building the Walls of Thebes with his Song, Orpheus claiming Eurydice from Hades, Hercules and the chained Cercopes, Bellerophon killing the Chimera*. In the fresco itself the sequence was rearranged, so that the last-named scene came between the first and second. Of the same date are three canvases formerly on the walls of the same room (now Da Schio collection, Castelgomberto, near Vicenza): *Ulysses discovering Achilles among the Daughters of Lycomedes, Hercules and Antaeus* and *Apollo and Marsyas*.

PROV. Private coll. Madrid; private coll., Zurich. Acquired Zurich 1959.

LIT. See *Catalogue* V.

106

Giovanni Battista Tiepolo (1696–1770)

106 *S. Aloysius (Luigi) Gonzaga in Glory*

Canvas. 58×44·7
Contemporary inscription on *verso*, 'Gio: Batta: Tiepolo 1735'
Inv. no.170

Aloysius Gonzaga (1568–1591), a Jesuit of noble birth who died young (patron saint of Catholic youth), was canonized in 1726. It has been suggested that the present picture, which corresponds in style with Tiepolo's work of about that date, was painted on this occasion; it appears to be a *modello* for an unexecuted altarpiece. The inscription on the back cannot refer to the date of execution, but may record the gift of the painting to the family of the sculptor, Andrea Fantoni, who had just made the frame for Tiepolo's altarpiece for the parish church at Rovetta (1734, installed 1736), and had died the same year (1734).

PROV. Presumably the family of Andrea Fantoni, from 1735; by descent at Casa Fantoni, Rovetta, near Bergamo. Acquired 1953.

EXH. R.A., 'European Masters of 18th cent.', 1954–5 (478); R.A., 'Italian Art', 1960 (411).

LIT. See *Catalogue* II and *Addenda*.

Giovanni Battista Tiepolo (1696–1770)

107 *The Madonna and Child with an Angel*

Canvas. 44·2×23·9; painted arched top
Inv. no.341

This small picture is related in style to the artist's early work, the 'Udine period' of c.1725–8; to the same early period belong Numbers 105 and 106 in this collection. The present painting had formerly been related to *The Madonna of the Rosary* of 1735 (Labia – formerly Robinson – collection, Cape Town), but is clearly a number of years earlier.

PROV. Jaffé coll., Berlin. Acquired 1964 from private coll., Bergamo.

LIT. See *Catalogue* V.

Giovanni Battista Tiepolo (1696–1770)

108 *S. Roch*

Canvas. 44×33
Inv. no.171

One of a numerous group of paintings of the same subject and format, generally dated to c.1730–35. They are assumed to have been painted for members of the Scuola di S. Rocco in Venice.

PROV. Baron von Stumm, Holzhausen, 1906 (?). Acquired 1952 from Count Zoubow, Paris.

EXH. R.A., 'Italian Art', 1960 (445).

LIT. See *Catalogue* II and *Addenda*.

107

108   109

Giovanni Battista Tiepolo (1696–1770)

109 *The Martyrdom of S. Clement*

Canvas. 58·5×32·5; within shaped border
Inv. no.395

For some time wrongly identified as S. John Nepomuk; papal attributes make
certain the saint's identity as Pope Clement of the first century, martyred by
drowning with an anchor. This painting is probably connected with the commission of the altarpiece, *The Trinity appearing to S. Clement* (*c*.1734–9), for the convent
church of the Trinity at Nymphenburg (now Munich, Alte Pinakothek), by
Archbishop-Elector Clement Augustus of Cologne. This is Tiepolo's only known
altarpiece of S. Clement and its shape corresponds with the shaped border of
Number 109, which may well be a preliminary *modello*, succeeded by that in the
National Gallery, London, which is close in composition though not in format to
the finished altarpiece. A close version of the present *modello* is in Bergamo
(Accademia Carrara).

PROV. Cheremetiev coll., Russia(?); Nicholson, London; J. Bass, sold Parke-
Bernet, New York, 25 Jan. 1945 (3); Sale, Sotheby, 24 June 1970 (34). Acquired
at sale.

LIT. See *Catalogue* VI; also: M. Levey, *Painting in Eighteenth-Century Venice*, 1959,
p.177 (2nd ed., 1980, pp.211, 249); subsequently: M. Levey, *National Gallery
Catalogues: The 17th and 18th Century Italian Schools*, 1971, pp.224–5; B. Heine in
Pantheon, XXXII, 1974, pp.149ff.

110

Giovanni Battista Tiepolo (1696–1770)

110 *The Martyrdom of S. Agatha*

Canvas. 48·3×29·1
Inv. no.396

Apparently a preliminary *modello* for Tiepolo's *Martyrdom of S. Agatha* in the Santo, Padua; the two compositions show considerable differences, but the relationship is confirmed by a second, similar-sized *modello* (Broglio coll., Paris), with likenesses to both, representing the intermediary stage of development towards Tiepolo's finished work (height *c*.3·5 m.). Documents suggest the date 1734 for the *modelli*; the altarpiece was completed by 1737; the project coincided approximately with that for *S. Clement* (Number 109).

PROV. Private coll., Vienna; Broglio coll., Paris, after 1945. Acquired London 1969.

EXH. Vienna, Gal. S. Lucas, 'Italienische Barockmalerei', 1937 (125).

LIT. See *Catalogue* VI.

Tiepolo and the Monastery Church of Aranjuez
(Numbers 111–116)

G. B. Tiepolo's last major commission was for seven altarpieces for S. Pascual, the monastery church of the Discalced Franciscans at Aranjuez, south of Madrid, built under royal patronage by Francesco Sabatini, 1765–70. All five known surviving *modelli* for the project are in this collection (111–115), as is a fragment of one of the altarpieces (116). Tiepolo received this commission in 1767, after five years at the court of Charles III of Spain, whose delegate for the present commission was his confessor Joaquin de Eleta. Eleta's hostility, it appears, and perhaps also the rivalry of Mengs and his followers caused difficulties and delay, and eventually the dispersal and in some cases the mutilation of the seven altarpieces. By 1769, and with the aid of Domenico Tiepolo, they were completed – subject to approval – but were not placed *in situ* until after Tiepolo's death in the following year. Antonio Ponz's *Viage de España* (1772) describes Tiepolo's altarpieces in the church, with the exception of *S. Charles Borromeo*, for which a crucifix had been substituted. Within a few years Tiepolo's work was replaced by that of Mengs, Bayeu and Maella, which survived apparently until the Civil War. The disposition of Tiepolo's altarpieces (*c*.2·75 m. high) can be reconstructed with the aid of Ponz's account: those represented by the present *modelli* were for the high altar (111, round-headed), the east walls of the transepts (112, 113, square-headed) and the second pair of low chapels in the nave (114, 115, round-headed). Where the upper part of an altarpiece survives its original shape can be traced, corresponding with the shape of its *modello*, and with its frame, still in the church. In the first pair of chapels at the entrance hung the two ovals whose *modelli* are untraced, showing the two Franciscan saints, *Anthony of Padua* (now Prado; the lost *modello* was once with the other five in Bayeu's collection, inv. no.145) and *Peter of Alcántara* (Madrid, Royal Palace), the 16th-century founder of the Spanish Discalced Franciscans.

Giovanni Battista Tiepolo (1696–1770)

111 *S. Paschal Baylon's Vision of the Eucharist*

Canvas. 63×38; within shaped border; internal measurement: 58×32·3
Inv. no.172
See introduction on p.75

Modello for the high altar of S. Pascual. Two large fragments of the altarpiece survive in the Prado, and the whole is recorded in an etching by Domenico Tiepolo, whose inscription indicates that it was his father's last work, completed in 1770. A drawing by G. B. Tiepolo of the angel holding the monstrance, in this collection (Number 184), must date after the *modello*: it shows the only significant change introduced in the finished altarpiece: the angel no longer holds the monstrance with the humeral veil prescribed for the priestly ritual of Mass. This change was perhaps requested by Padre Eleta after the initial completion of the altarpiece in 1769. S. Paschal, a 16th-century Spanish Discalced Franciscan and titular saint of the church, whose monastic occupation as gardener is alluded to in the painting, was noted for his devotion to the cult of the Sacrament and saw in a vision angels presenting the Eucharist in a monstrance.

PROV. Francisco Bayeu (1734–95; Goya's brother-in-law), inv. no.133; acquired from his executors by Leonardo Chopinot; Hulot coll., 1800, sold, G. Petit, Paris, 10 May 1892 (141); Private coll., Brazil. Acquired Milan 1937.

EXH. Venice, 'Tiepolo', 1951 (98); R. A., 'European 18th century', 1954–5 (500); R.A., 'Italian Art', 1960 (412).

LIT. See *Catalogue* II and *Addenda*; also: *Catalogue* 1937 (22); M. Levey, *Painting in Eighteenth-Century Venice*, 1959, pp.202f. (2nd ed., 1980, pp.236f); M. Levey in *Burlington Magazine*, CII, 1960, p.123; subsequently: G. Knox, *Giambattista and Domenico Tiepolo. A Study and 'Catalogue Raisonné' of the Chalk Drawings*, 1980, I, pp.246, 328.

Giovanni Battista Tiepolo (1696–1770)

112 *The Immaculate Conception*

Canvas. 63·5×38·5; within shaped border;   COLOUR PLATE XVI
internal measurement: 56×30
Inv. no.342
See introduction on p.75

Modello for the altarpiece in the north transept of S. Pascual, which is preserved intact in the Prado. The neutral surround of the *modello* was previously folded over the stretcher, resulting in partial loss and damage. The Franciscans were among the chief protagonists of the dogma of the Immaculate Conception of the Virgin.

PROV. Francisco Bayeu (1734–95), inv. no.135; acquired from his executors by Leonardo Chopinot; 9th Lord Kinnaird, by whom probably acquired, at Rossie Priory by 1826. Acquired from Lord Kinnaird 1967.

EXH. R.A., 'European 18th Century', 1954–5 (498); R.A., 'Goya and his Times', 1963–4 (5).

LIT. See *Catalogue* V; also: Marques del Saltillo, in *Miscelanea Madrileña, Historica y Artistica*, I, 1952, p.76 (135); M. Levey, *loc. cit.* under Number 111; subsequently: G. Knox, *loc. cit.*, p.328.

112

113

Giovanni Battista Tiepolo (1696–1770)

113 *The Stigmatization of S. Francis*

Canvas. 63×38; within shaped border; internal measurement: 55·5×30·5
Inv. no.173
See introduction on p.75

Modello for the altarpiece in the south transept of S. Pascual, which is now in the Prado, intact and signed 'Dn Juan Tiepolo inv. et pinx.' The changes in the finished painting include the elimination of the Cross and the praying Franciscan (brother Leo) on the left, and a more conventional upward gaze of the saint. Faint indications in the *modello* suggest that this may initially have been round-headed.

PROV. as for Number 111 (Bayeu inv. no.138).

EXH. as for Number 111: 1951 (99); 1954–5 (507); 1960 (419).

LIT. as for Number 111 (no.23 in *Catalogue* 1937; Knox, *op. cit.*, p.328.

114

Giovanni Battista Tiepolo (1696–1770)

114 *S. Joseph with the Christ Child*

Canvas. 63×38; within shaped border; internal measurement: 56·5×32
Inv. no.174
See introduction on p.75

Modello for the altarpiece in the second chapel on the left in S. Pascual. Three fragments of this now mutilated altarpiece survive: the largest shows the central group (Detroit, Institute of Arts); two smaller fragments show angels (Prado; this collection, Number 116). A unique record of the whole, showing considerable differences from the *modello*, is a drawing, squared for transfer, by Domenico Tiepolo (Vevey, Musée Jenisch). The subject, cultivated by S. Teresa, was especially favoured in Spain.

PROV. Francisco Bayeu (1734–95), inv. no.137; acquired from his executors by Leonardo Chopinot; South American collection(?). Acquired London 1949.

EXH. As for Number 111: 1951 (101); 1954–5 (501); 1960 (414).

LIT. See *Catalogue* II and *Addenda*; also: M. Levey, *loc. cit.* under Number 111; subsequently: G. Knox, *op. cit.*, pp.194, 328.

115

Giovanni Battista Tiepolo (1696–1770)

115 *S. Charles Borromeo meditating on the Crucifix*

Canvas. 63×38; within shaped border; internal measurement: 56×31·3
Inv. no.175
See introduction on p.75

Modello for the altarpiece in the second chapel on the right in S. Pascual. Of the altarpiece only a fragment survives, a half-length of the saint with the crucifix (Cincinnati Art Museum); no significant differences from the *modello* can be seen there, but the *modello*'s visible correction in the figure of the saint appears unusual for Tiepolo. S. Charles Borromeo, 16th-century archbishop of Milan, was Cardinal Protector of the Franciscan Order; a hospital dedicated to him (1776; chapel 1778) was built opposite the convent of S. Pascual.

PROV. As for Number 114 (Bayeu inv. no.139).

EXH. As for Number 111: 1951 (100); 1954–5 (508); 1960 (417).

LIT. As for Number 114 (Knox, *op. cit.*, pp.269, 328).

116

Giovanni Battista Tiepolo (1696–1770)

116 *Two Heads of Angels* (fragment)

Canvas. 50·8×41·5
Inv. no.343
See introduction on p.75

Fragment of the altarpiece of *S. Joseph with the Christ Child*, from the second chapel on the left in S. Pascual, of which two other fragments survive (Detroit Institute of Arts; Prado, Madrid). The composition of the *modello* (Number 114 in this collection, q.v.) was considerably altered for the finished painting, recorded in Domenico Tiepolo's drawing. This shows that, although Number 116 and the Prado *Angel* at one time constituted a single fragment, they were not originally contiguous. There is speculation on the authorship of each of the finished altarpieces, but the quality of this fragment suggests G. B. Tiepolo rather than Domenico.

PROV. (Larger fragment, before division): Eugenio Lucas; Rafael García Palencia, Madrid; Tomás Harris, London (1928/9); F. Rothmann, Berlin; Caspari, Munich; Frey, Paris (who probably separated the two fragments). *Angel with a Wreath*: sold Paris 1933, acquired by Prado. Number 116: various dealers. Acquired Rome 1959.

LIT. See *Catalogue* v and *Addenda*; subsequently: G. Knox, *op. cit.* under Number 111, p.328.

117

118

119

Jacopo Tintoretto (1518–1594)

117 *Esther before Ahasuerus*

Canvas. 17×48·5
Inv. no.76

One of a number of *cassoni* paintings, including Numbers 118 and 119 and a series of six, much longer panels (*c.* 1·5 m.) in Vienna (Kunsthistorisches Museum), all thought to date from the 1540s. The present picture differs from these in being the smallest, on canvas, and, apparently, slightly earlier in date – in style still reminiscent of Bonifazio dei Pitati. Like the others in this group, it was previously attributed to Andrea Schiavone. The Old Testament subject of the Jewess, Esther, interceding for her people with Ahasuerus (Xerxes) is from *Esther*, V, 1–2 *et seq.*

PROV. Sale, Christie's, 14 Mar. 1952 (69, as Andrea Schiavone). Acquired at sale.

LIT. See *Catalogue* II; subsequently: C. Bernari and P. de Vecchi, *L'Opera completa del Tintoretto*, 1970, p.88 (21).

Jacopo Tintoretto (1518–1594)

118 *Latona changing the Lycian Peasants into Frogs*

Panel. 22·9×65·8
Inv. no.77

One of a group of *cassoni* panels from the 1540s, which includes Number 117 (q.v.) and 119. The present picture and Number 119 (both Forbes coll. in 1936), are of similar size, on thick panel and rough in handling, and must be from the same piece of furniture or decorative scheme. A comparable panel in the National Gallery, *Jupiter and Semele* (22×65·4 cm.) also appears to belong with them. For the subject, from Ovid, see Number 33.

PROV. William Forbes of Medwyn; Miss Dorothy Forbes, sold Christie's, 17 April 1936 (4, as by Andrea Schiavone); bought Davis. Acquired London 1953.

EXH. Edinburgh(?) 'Old Masters and Scottish National Portraits', 1883.

LIT. C. Bernari and P. de Vecchi, *L'Opera completa del Tintoretto*, 1970, p.88 (23).

Jacopo Tintoretto (1518–1594)

119 *Apollo and Diana killing the Children of Niobe*

Panel. 22·9×67·7
Inv. no.337

Companion *cassone* panel to Number 118 (q.v.). The subject, from Ovid (*Metamorphoses*, VI, 218ff.), is Apollo and Diana's revenge on the Theban queen Niobe, who claimed superiority over their mother, Latona (Leto); they kill her seven sons and seven daughters.

PROV. Miss Dorothy Forbes, sold Christie's, 17 April 1936 (40, as by Andrea Schiavone); bought Asscher. Acquired London 1964.

EXH. Colnaghi, 'Old Masters', 1964 (9).

120

Jacopo and Domenico Tintoretto (1518–1594 and 1560–1635)

120 *The Adoration of the Shepherds*

Canvas. 75·2×85·7
Inv. no.78

Probably a work of collaboration. Jacopo seems to have left to his son the painting of such details as the animals and the 'still life' in the foreground. This picture is thought to date from the same period as the *Adoration of the Shepherds* in the Upper Hall of the Scuola di San Rocco in Venice – the second half of the 1570s – where the principles of composition and use of light are similar. X-rays reveal changes during execution in some areas, including the figure of the Virgin.

PROV. Douglas Freshfield (1921); J. Seymour Maynard, sold Christie's, 29 Jan. 1954 (42, as Jacopo Bassano). Acquired London 1954.

EXH. Burlington Fine Arts Club, 1934 (73, as Venetian, mid–16th cent.).

LIT. See *Catalogue* II; subsequently: C. Bernari and P. de Vecchi, *L'Opera completa del Tintoretto*, 1970, p.134 (A.5, as doubtful attribution).

121

Titian(?) (1477/89–1576)

121 *Cameria, Daughter of Suleiman the Magnificent, as S. Catherine*

Canvas. 102·5×76·5
Inv. no.331

This appears to be a version, possibly autograph, of Titian's lost 'portrait' of Cameria (or Camelia), recorded by Vasari (1568 edit.). The identity of the figure is based on her close likeness to inscribed copies after the portrait in Paolo Giovio's celebrated collection at Como. J. Wilde (in *Catalogue* V), who suggested a date of *c.*1555 for the present painting, proposed that Giovio's prime version was Titian's lost, imaginary, portrait, seen by Vasari; it seems more probable that Titian himself copied from a true likeness in Giovio's *musaeum* – where authenticity was the rule. (For the similar case of Titian's lost *Cortez* see under Number 62.) The 'conversion' of Cameria – who married the Grand Vizier Rustem Pasha in 1544 – into S. Catherine, by the addition of a wheel, is mystifying. Titian's authorship of this version has recently been doubted.

PROV. Baron Ricciardi; Dr. A. Walter, Naples, exhib. Munich, May 1896, sold 4 June 1896 (108); Sale, Berlin, 1899; Baroness Katharina Kiss-Schratt, Vienna; gift to her son, Baron Anton Kiss. Acquired from Baron Kiss 1938.

LIT. See *Catalogue* V; subsequently: H. E. Wethey, *The Paintings of Titian*, II. *The Portraits*, 1971, pp.190f. (L–2).

van Dyck: see Dyck

122

Franz Wiegele (1887–1944)

122 *Young Woman in a Landscape (Carinthia)*

Canvas. 42×50
Inv. no.261

Painted some time before 1938 by this artist of the Austrian 'Nötsch' School, whose centre was the village of Nötsch in Carinthia. A fellow member of this group of artists was Sebastian Isepp (1884–1954), restorer of the paintings in this collection; also associated was Gerhart Frankl (see Number 29).

PROV. Presented by the artist to Mrs. Gerhart Frankl. Acquired 1949 as a gift from Gerhart Frankl.

Marco Zoppo (1432–1478)

123 *S. Sebastian in a Rocky Landscape with SS. Jerome, Anthony Abbot and Christopher*

Panel. 41·9×31·4
On the back an old inscription, 'Andrea Mantegna Pinxit', and a label, 'Mr Skippe No.4'
Inv. no.71

A well-preserved panel exemplifying Zoppo's late style. The rock formations and rendering of the nude are characteristic of the artist; in addition, the influence of Mantegna is apparent and that of Antonello da Messina is suggested by the colours, and by the attempt at suggesting distance. Its experimental character in terms of space is confirmed by recent technical research (by Paula De Cristofaro), which revealed the underdrawing of a large tree reaching to the cloud on the left. Zoppo, of Bolognese origin, appears to have been in Venice from the 1460s. Antonello arrived there in 1475 and the present painting may be datable to 1475–8.

PROV. Venice, 18th century; purchased in Venice by John Skippe; H. Hanbury-Martin; H. E. Benn. Acquired London 1951.

LIT. See *Addenda;* subsequently: L. Armstrong, *The Paintings and Drawings of Marco Zoppo*, 1976, pp.134ff., 388 (23).

123

Drawings
Selection A (Cat. Nos.124 to 153)

124

Fra Bartolommeo (1472–1517)

124 *The Sweep of a River with Fishermen and a Town in the Background*

Pen and ink. 21·1×29
Inv. no.88

The sheet was previously bound with forty others by the same artist (many drawn on both sides), including six more in this collection (see 154 in Selection B). The album, consisting of landscapes and nature studies, was assembled in 1730 by Gabburri (see PROV.) and split up for the 1957 Sotheby sale. One at least (inv. no.83, not on exhibition) was used for a painting designed by Fra Bartolommeo. They probably all date after 1504 when he resumed his career as a painter at S. Marco, Florence.

PROV. In the artist's studio after his death; Fra Paolina da Pistoia; Suor Plautilla Nelli; Convent of S. Catherine in Piazza San Marco, Florence; Cavaliere Francesco Maria Nicolo Gabburri (1675–1742); William Kent(?); private coll., Ireland (?); Sale, Sotheby, 20 Nov. 1957 (36). Acquired at sale.

LIT. See *Catalogue* II and *Addenda*.

125

Giovanni Bellini (*c*.1430–1516)

125 *The Nativity*

Pen and ink slightly washed, both upper corners cut. 20·1×21·2
Inscribed 'L' by a later hand, lower right.
Inv. no.79

One of the few surviving composition studies by Bellini. Because of the scarcity of his drawings their attribution has been much debated. This *Nativity*, however, seems certainly to be autograph, dating from *c*.1475. The use of the broken pen-line was apparently Bellini's innovation (see Wilde, under LIT.).

PROV. Sir Peter Lely (Lugt 2092); George Le Hunte; The Misses Le Hunte, sold Sotheby, 9 June 1955 (43). Acquired at sale.

LIT. See *Addenda;* subsequently: J. Wilde, *Venetian Art from Bellini to Titian*, 1974, pp.26f.

126

Pieter Bruegel the Elder (*c*.1525–1569)

126 *Landscape with an Artist sketching*

Pen and ink with faint traces of black chalk. 27·7×39·6
Inscribed, lower left, in 16th-cent.(?) hand, 'de ouden Breugel', and on the *verso*,
'den ouden Breugel no.56'.
Inv. no.9

Bruegel's alpine landscape drawings appear to have been drawn mainly in the
studio in the mid-1550s, with the aid of chalk studies made during his passage
through the Alps on his journeys to and from Italy (*c*.1551–4). Recently, a date of
c.1552–3, during his sojourn in Italy, has been proposed for the group. The
majority of the alpine drawings (including three more in this collection) are not,
apparently, of identifiable places, but are skilful collections of motifs which
reappear also in a number of his series of engraved alpine landscapes. The
inclusion of the figure of an artist sketching is rare and significant for the period.

PROV. possibly Georg Hoefnagel (1542–1600); in England *c*.1800, when bound in
album including inv. no.8 (not on exhibition); album split up by 1948. Acquired
London 1948.

LIT. See *Catalogue* I and *Addenda*; subsequently: F. Grossmann in exh. cat., *Bruegel:
Une dynastie de peintres*, Brussels, Palais des Beaux-Arts, 1980, p.29, and K.
Oberhuber in the same, p.65; M. Gibson, *Bruegel*, 1980, pp.15, 90f., 178.

127

Pieter Bruegel the Elder (*c.*1525/30–1569)

127 *View of Antwerp from the Sea*

Pen and ink with faint traces of black chalk. 20·3×30
Laid down
Inscribed, not by the artist, lower left: 'Breughel'.
Inv. no.11

The drawing, at one time placed at the start of Bruegel's career, is now considered a more mature work of *c.*1559. It has been suggested that the city of Antwerp may be portrayed allegorically: the ships appear to be sailing from sunshine into the storm and the tiny island in the foreground is occupied only by the gallows.

PROV. Acquired 1936 from Sir Bruce Ingram.

EXH. Brussels, 'Cinq Siècles d'Art', 1935 (433); Colnaghi, 'Masters of Maritime Art. A loan exhibition of Drawings from the Collection of Capt. Bruce S. Ingram', 1936 (82).

LIT. See *Catalogue* 1 and *Addenda*.

128

Pieter Bruegel the Elder (*c.*1525/30–1569)

128 *Landscape with two Peasants and a Dog*

Pen and ink over black chalk. 19·4×31
Signed and dated, lower left, 'bruegel 1562'.
Inv. no.317

At least five other landscape drawings by the artist, of nearly identical dimensions, are signed and dated to the same year. Three are views of Amsterdam; all show a view more confined and intimate in scale than the great alpine views of the 1550s.

PROV. Charles Hanbury Williams, M.P.; Sale, Sotheby, 26 June 1957 (4). Acquired London 1957.

LIT. See *Catalogue* IV.

Giovanni Antonio Canal, called Canaletto (1697–1768)

129 *A View from Somerset Gardens looking towards London Bridge*

Pen and brown ink and grey washes. 23·4×72·8
Inv. no.131

The view starts from the terrace of Old Somerset House and, from S. Paul's to London Bridge in the distance, embraces a considerable array of the City churches. This extensive panorama was probably constructed with the aid of copious studies made from various sites, rather than with the use of a *camera obscura*, as was previously supposed. Canaletto spent ten years in England, from 1746, apart from brief returns to Venice. The present drawing is perhaps the earliest of the artist's versions of this view; others include a smaller drawing and a painting in the Royal coll., and a painting in the Mellon coll. which was engraved.

129

PROV. Slade sale, 1801; Mrs. Heywood Johnstone, sold Christie's, 20 Feb. 1925 (20), bought Ellis and Smith; 1929, A. Fauchier Magnan, sold Sotheby, 4 Dec. 1935 (3). Acquired at sale.

EXH. R.A., 'Italian Art', 1960 (634).

LIT. See *Catalogue* II and *Addenda*; subsequently: W. G. Constable, *Canaletto* (revised J. G. Links), 1976, pp.143, 418, 421, 575 (no.745); exh. cat., *Canaletto*, The Queens Gallery, 1980–81, under nos.38, 86.

Giovanni Antonio Canal, called Canaletto (1697–1768)

130 *The Piazza di S. Giacomo di Rialto*

Pencil, pen and brown ink and grey washes. 31·8×43·3
Signed, lower left, 'Antonio Canal del.'
Inscribed by the artist, below, on joined paper, 'Piazza di S. Giaccomo di Rialto in Venezia, con parte del Famoso Ponte in distanza, Versso S. Bartolm:^{co}'
Inv. no.132

A drawing evidently made, like Number 129, as an independent work of art, and preserved in remarkably fresh condition. Its style and rich technique indicate a late date, in the 1760s. There are four other versions of the view by Canaletto of different dates: a drawing (Berlin, Print Room), two paintings (Dresden and Ottawa) and an engraving. Changes in the appearance of the buildings represented in the scene indicate that the artist used earlier sketches as well as up-to-date ones to compose the present view.

PROV. Marquis de Lagoy (Lugt 1710); Samuel Woodburn (?); Thomas Dinsdale (Lugt 2426 on *verso*); Sir John Leslie; Sale, Gilhofer and Ranschburg, Lucerne, 28 June 1934 (66). Acquired at sale.

EXH. Munich, J. Böhler, 'Altvenezianische Malerei', 1931 (63).

LIT. See *Catalogue* II and *Addenda*; also: M. Levey in *Burlington Magazine*, CII, 1960, p.123; subsequently: W. G. Constable, *Canaletto* (revised J. G. Links), 1976, pp.167, 335f., 517 (no.611).

Piazza di S. Giacomo di Rialto in Venezia, con parte del famoso Ponte in distanza, Verso S. Bartolm.

130

131

Vittore Carpaccio (*c.*1455–1525/6)

131 *The Virgin reading to the Infant Christ*

Pen and ink over red chalk. 12·8×9·4
On the *verso:* The Virgin adoring the Infant Christ, with S. John; the design severely cut on the left.
Inv. no.82

Both *recto* and *verso* of this sheet record what are, apparently, the artist's first ideas for compositions which he himself was to paint more than once and which were influential on Venetian painting in general. The *verso* appears to be a study for a signed painting in Frankfurt (Städelsches Kunstinstitut), the *recto* a study for a painting in Washington (National Gallery of Art), which is now cut on the left and entitled *A Saint Reading*. The figures were repeated in Carpaccio's later works. An early date, *c.*1490, has been proposed for the drawing.

PROV. Sir Thomas Lawrence (Lugt 2445 on *verso*); Samuel Woodburn, sold Christie's, 4ff June 1860, no.2 (10); Sir Thomas Phillipps; by descent, T. Fitzroy Phillipps Fenwick. Acquired with the Fenwick coll., 1946.

EXH. Victoria and Albert Museum, 'Drawing: Technique and Purpose', 1981 (119).

LIT. See *Catalogue* II and *Addenda;* also: M. Levey in *Burlington Magazine*, CII, 1960, p.123; subsequently: T. Pignatti, *Vittore Carpaccio*, 1972, pp.9, 14, 19 (as formerly in this collection); M. Muraro, *I Disegni di Vittore Carpaccio*, 1977, pp.64f. (as New York, Wildenstein).

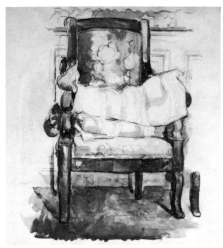

132

133

Paul Cézanne (1839–1906)

132 *An Armchair*

Pencil and watercolour. 32·2×33·8
Faint numerals and inscription, lower left.
Inv. no.238

COLOUR PLATE XXIV

A striking watercolour probably of *c*.1885–90. Its subject suggests comparison with van Gogh's *Chair*, painted at Arles in 1888 (London, National Gallery). There is a pencil study, present whereabouts unknown, apparently of the same chair with a cushion, dated to *c*.1887 by Chappuis (*The Drawings of Paul Cézanne*, 1973, no.960).

PROV. A. Vollard, Paris. Acquired 1937 from Simon Meller.

LIT. See *Catalogue* III.

Paul Cézanne (1839–1906)

133 *Madame Cézanne sewing*

Pencil. 47·4×31
Laid down
Inv. no.239

This portrait is of Hortense Fiquet, whom Cézanne met in 1869, lived with in the following year and married in 1886. It is usually dated to the period immediately after their marriage, although sometimes considered to be earlier, *c*.1880. Reproduced as the frontispiece in Vollard's monograph on the artist, 1914.

PROV. A. Vollard, Paris; H. von Simolin, Berlin; Paul Cassirer. Acquired London 1941.

EXH. Rotterdam, Boymans Museum, 'Ingres à Seurat', 1933–4 (5); Amsterdam, Paul Cassirer, 'Fransche Meesters uit de XIXᶜ Eeuw', 1938 (20); Arts Council, Hayward Gallery, 'Cézanne Drawings', 1973 (66).

LIT. See *Catalogue* III; subsequently: W. Anderson, *Cézanne's Portrait Drawings*, 1970, no.67; A. Chappuis, *The Drawings of Paul Cézanne*, 1973, no.729; L. Venturi, *Cézanne*, 1978, pp.76, 81. (Present location not known to these authors.)

Claude Gellée, called Claude Lorrain (1600–1682)

134 *Study for 'The Arrival of Aeneas at Pallanteum'*

Graphite, pen and brown ink and two shades of brown wash; corrections in white body-colour. 17·7×25·2
Signed and dated, lower left, 'Roma 1675 Claudio fecit'. Inscribed over the hills to left and right (where partly obscured by white body-colour) with names of places mentioned in the *Aeneid*. Squared with diagonals and surrounded with frame-line.
Inv. no.215

Study for the picture in the Fairhaven coll. (National Trust, Anglesey Abbey), painted 1675 for Don Gasparo Altieri. The diagonals were an aid for transferring the design to canvas. There are seven further preparatory drawings for the painting. The date on the present one must have been added later by the artist, after wiping away some of the wash; the drawing is probably *c*.1673. The subject is from Virgil's *Aeneid*, Book VIII. Aeneas is arriving on the banks of the Tiber

134

below the Aventine Hill, left; on the right are the hill-towns of Janiculum and Saturnia.

PROV. Odescalchi, before 1700; by descent until 1958, when bought and sold by Calmann; from the album now in the Norton Simon coll. Acquired London 1958.

EXH. Arts Council, Hayward Gallery, 'Claude Lorrain', 1969 (108).

LIT. See *Catalogue* III and *Addenda*.

Jean Honoré Fragonard (1732–1806)

135 *'La Résignée'; the Artist's Daughter, Rosalie (?)*

Red chalk. 22·5×17·2
Laid down
Signed and dated, lower left, 'frago 1785'
Inv. no.229
The date, which has been misread as 1765, was given correctly as 1785 when

135

etched by Jules de Goncourt for the book on Fragonard of 1865. In a communica-
tion from Eunice Williams, who drew attention to the correct reading of the date
in relation to the style of the drawing, the sitter is convincingly identified as the
artist's daughter, Rosalie. She died of consumption in 1788, at the age of 18,
which would explain the attitude of weakness seen here and in the other drawings
of the same sitter identified by Eunice Williams.

PROV. M. Marcille senior, 1857; E. and J. de Goncourt (Lugt 1089), sold Paris
15ff. Feb. 1897 (83); P. Decourcelle, sold G. Petit, Paris, 29f. May 1911 (89);
E. M. Hodgkins, sold G. Petit, Paris, 30 April 1914 (26); Sale, Sotheby, 9 Dec.
1936 (50). Acquired at sale (?).

EXH. Paris, École des Beaux-Arts, 'Dessins des maîtres anciens', 1879 (593);
Paris, Gal. G. Petit, 'Chardin – Fragonard', 1907 (169 bis); Berlin, Königliche
Kunstakademie, 'L'art français au XVIIIᵉ siècle', 1910 (172; German cat., 199);
R. A., 'France in 18th-cent.', 1968 (258).

LIT. See *Catalogue* III and *Addenda*.

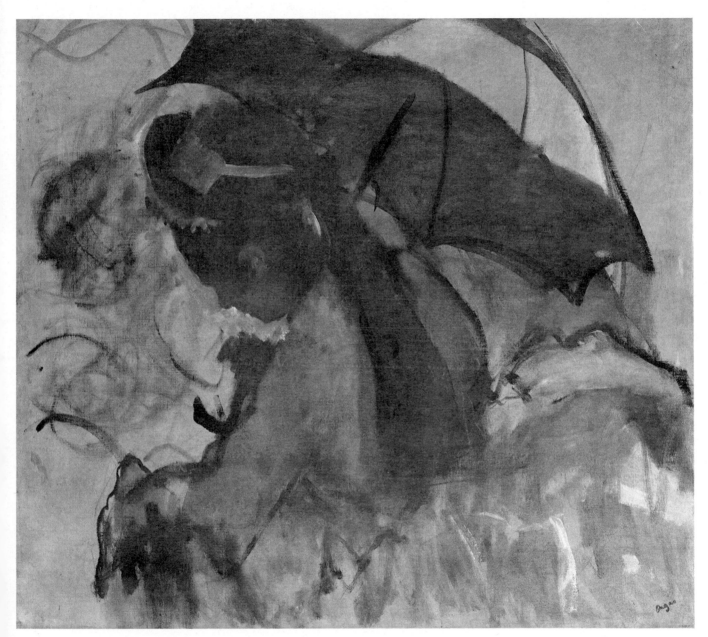

PLATE XVII Edgar Degas *Lady with a Parasol* cat.16

PLATE XVIII Paul Cézanne *'Route Tournante'* CAT.10

136

Francesco Guardi (1712–1793)

136 *The Feast of Ascension Day*

Pen and ink and wash over black chalk. 19·6×38·8
Inv. no.138

At the annual feast day recorded here the Doge rode out to the Lido in the State Barge, the 'Bucintoro' (seen setting out, near the centre), to perform the marriage ritual between Venice and the sea. The church of S. Maria della Salute is indicated faintly on the right in chalk. There are paintings and drawings by Guardi showing different views of the same annual ceremony. The present drawing has been dated to the early 1780s, but Morassi (1975, see LIT.) places it among Guardi's latest works.

PROV. E. Warneck, Paris, sold Paris, 10f. May 1905 (177); Marius Paulme (Lugt 1910), sold G. Petit, Paris, 11ff May 1929 (100), bought R. Owen. Acquired New York 1950.

LIT. See *Catalogue* II and *Addenda*; subsequently: A. Morassi, *Guardi. Tutti i Disegni*, 1975, no.280.

Lorenzo Lotto(?) (*c*.1480–1556)

137 *Portrait of a Young Man*

Black chalk, heightened with white and with red on the lips, on green prepared ground. 33·5×29·9
Inv. no.90

The artist himself probably rubbed or washed the chalk in the cap; the lightly-

137

drawn hair on the left has faded. The attribution of this fine portrait drawing to
Lotto has generally been accepted without reservation, and only doubted in
Catalogue II because of the lack of comparable drawings by the artist. It appears to
be related to Lotto's early painted portraits of *c.*1508–10.

PROV. William Russell; Henry Wagner; A. G. B. Russell (Lugt, *Suppl.*, 2770a),
sold Sotheby, 9 June 1955 (6). Acquired at sale.

EXH. Agnew (Artists' General Benevolent Fund), 1925 (119); R.A., 'Italian Art',
1930 (601); Paris, Petit Palais, 'L'Art Italien', 1935 (589); R.A. (Diploma Gallery), 'Drawings by Old Masters', 1953 (85).

LIT. See *Catalogue* II; subsequently: R. Pallucchini and G. Mariani Canova,
L'Opera completa del Lotto, 1975, p.122 (276).

138

Michelangelo (1475–1564)

138 *The Virgin and Child*

Pen and brown ink over red chalk. 16·5×7·5
Laid down
Inscribed, lower edge, with the artist's name and dates, and, top left, with numerals (?)
Inv. no.421 (not in *Catalogue*)

The drawing has been dated by Michael Hirst to *c.*1516. He has suggested a connection with the statue of the Virgin and Child proposed at that time for the tomb of Julius II (see 1975 exh. cat.).

PROV. Acquired London 1970.

EXH. British Museum, 'Michelangelo', 1975 (33).

Michelangelo (1475–1564)

139 *'The Dream of Human Life'*

Black chalk, stippled. 39·6×27·9
Inv. no.424 (not in *Catalogue*)

Now established as Michelangelo's celebrated original, of which there are numerous copies, engraved, drawn and painted (e.g., National Gallery, no.8). It is one of a number of 'presentation drawings', of extremely refined technique, made by the artist for his particular friends. The recipient of *The Dream*, which is datable to *c*.1533, is unknown. The central figure, reclining on the terrestrial globe, repeats that in Sebastiano del Piombo's *Raising of Lazarus* (*c*.1516–19, National Gallery), designed with Michelangelo's assistance. The title 'Il Sogno' was given by Vasari (1568). No contemporary explanation of the allegory survives and various interpretations of the subject have been suggested. One, which derives from a description of 1642, and echoes Neoplatonic theory, explains that the Human Mind is being re-awakened by the trumpeting angel to the celestial sphere and to Virtue, banishing the Vices (represented by the surrounding arc of six of the Seven Deadly Sins) and the illusions (the masks beneath) of Man's 'dream' or 'exile' on earth. The flying figure is more often interpreted as Fame, recalling the mind from sinful or wasteful preoccupations. (Unpublished notes by J. Wilde used for this entry.)

PROV. Casa Buonarroti; J. B. J. Wicar (these two according to Woodburn); W. Y. Ottley, sold London, 23 June 1814 (1767); Sir Thomas Lawrence (Lugt 2445); Samuel Woodburn in 1836; William II of Holland, sold The Hague, Aug. 1850, bought Woodburn; by 1875, Grand Duke of Saxe-Weimar. Acquired 1952 from the Grand Duke Carl August of Saxe-Weimar.

EXH. Woodburn Gall., 'The Lawrence Gallery. . . Tenth Exhibition', 1836 (77; '. . . it is one of the finest drawings in the world'); British Museum, 'Michelangelo', 1953 (74); R.A., 'Italian Art', 1960 (541); British Museum, 'Michelangelo', 1975 (128).

LIT. G. F. Waagen, *Works of Art and Artists in England*, 1838, II, p.172; K. Frey, *Die Handzeichnungen Michelagniolos Buonarroti*, 1909–11, text, p.76; H. Thode, *Michelangelo. Kritische Untersuchungen über seine Werke*, III, 1913, no.520; B. Berenson, *The Drawings of the Florentine Painters*, 2nd ed., 1938, no.1748B; E. Panofsky, *Studies in Iconology*, 1939, pp.223ff.; L. Goldscheider, *Michelangelo Drawings*, 1951, no.93; J. Wilde, *Italian Drawings. . . in the British Museum. Michelangelo and his Studio*, 1953, p.95; L. Dussler, *Die Zeichnungen des Michelangelo*, 1959, no.589; C. de Tolnay, *Michelangelo*, V, 1960, no.169; F. Hartt, *Michelangelo Drawings*, 1971, no.359; C. de Tolnay, *Corpus dei Disegni di Michelangelo*, II, 1976, no.333; J. Wilde, *Michelangelo*, 1978, p.153.

139

140

Girolamo Francesco Maria Mazzola, called Parmigianino (1503–1540)

140 *Venus disarming Cupid*

Black chalk on pink-tinted paper, heightened with white. 17·4×14
Laid down
Inscribed, lower left, in an old hand, 'Parmesan', and, near the centre, '50' (?)
Inv. no.364

Parmigianino made a number of studies of this subject, in a variety of poses and technique, all considered to date from *c.*1527–30, the artist's years in Bologna.

PROV. Nathaniel Hillier (?); Sir Joshua Reynolds (Lugt 2364); John Brophy. Acquired London 1960.

EXH. Colnaghi, 'Old Master Drawings', 1960 (3).

LIT. See *Catalogue* v and *Addenda*; also: John Brophy, *The Mind's Eye*, 1949, p.20; subsequently: A. E. Popham, *Catalogue of the Drawings of Parmigianino*, 1971, no.766.

141

Pablo Picasso (1881–1973)

141 *Female Nude with her Arm resting on a Chair*

Charcoal, rubbed. 32×24·6
Signed, 'Picasso'
On the *verso*, in pencil, a cubist design with two standing figures, and the numerals '582'
Inv. no.265

The drawing is datable to *c.*1920–21, a period characterized by numerous paintings and drawings of monumental and classical female figures, which Picasso produced at the same time as his cubist works.

PROV. Acquired London 1941.

Rembrandt van Rijn (1606–1669)

142 *The Artist's Wife, Saskia, standing and holding a Flower in her right Hand; full-length*

Pen and brush and ink. 22·8×15·2   COLOUR PLATE XXI
Inv. no.405

A portrait considered to date from around the time of the artist's marriage in 1634 to Saskia van Ulenborch. The drawing, rich and striking in appearance, presents a poignant contrast to later studies of Saskia as the ailing mother of short-lived children. She died in 1642.

PROV. Acquired 1962 from Hugh Squire.

EXH. Colnaghi, 'Old Master Drawings', 1962 (31).

LIT. see *Catalogue* VI.

142

143

Rembrandt van Rijn (1606–1669)

143 *Saskia with one of her Children*

Red chalk. 14·1×10·6
Inv. no.183

This is almost certainly a portrait of the artist's wife with one of her first two children, Rumbartus (1635–6) or Cornelia I (1638), both of whom lived only for a month or two. The style of the drawing, suggesting a date of *c.*1636–8, seems to exclude the identification of the baby with Cornelia II (1640) or Titus, born 1641, the only one to survive childhood.

PROV. James Harris (?); The Earl of Malmesbury; Viscount Fitzharris, sold Christie's, 21 April 1950 (95). Acquired London 1950.

LIT. see *Catalogue* III and *Addenda*.

Rembrandt van Rijn (1606–1669)

144 *The Holy Family in the Carpenter's Shop*

Pen and ink and wash with traces of white body-colour. 18·2×23·4
Inv. no.193

The theme of the Holy Family in a domestic setting is found particularly in Rembrandt's paintings and drawings of the 1640s. The present sheet has been dated on grounds of style to *c.*1646.

PROV. Alexander Irvine of Dunn; Hugh Irvine; Margaret Irvine; Capt. Douglas Wimberley; Maj.-Gen. Douglas Wimberley. Acquired London 1953.

LIT. see *Catalogue* III and *Addenda*.

144

145

Rembrandt van Rijn (1606–1669)

145 *View of Diemen*

Pen and ink and wash. 8·8×15·5
On the *verso*, numbers in red ink (see PROV.), and 'Diemen van Rembrandt
f 2–10–' in red chalk, written in an old hand
Inv. no.199

A number of other drawings by Rembrandt are known of the village of Diemen,
near Amsterdam; all, including the present sheet, are thought to date from
around 1650. Doubts once expressed about the authenticity of the washes in this
drawing seem to be dispelled by careful examination and by consideration of the
'finished' nature of the work.

PROV. J. Pz. Zoomer (1641–1724; Lugt 1511); V. Röver (1686–1739; Lugt, *Suppl.*,
2984 on *verso*) ?; Jhr. J. Goll van Franckenstein, father (1722–85) and son
(1756–1821; Lugt 2987 on *verso*), sold Amsterdam, 1ff. July 1833 (N3035 –
inscribed in red ink on *verso*); Cranenburg coll.; Heimsoeth coll., sold Frankfurt,
1879; Dr. A. Straeter (Lugt 787 on *verso*), sold Gutekunst, Stuttgart, 1off. May
1898 (1180); Atherton Curtis (Lugt 94 on *verso*), sold Klipstein, Berne, 28 April
1955 (372). Acquired at sale.

EXH. Mount Kisco, New York, 'Prints and Drawings by Rembrandt in Curtis
coll.', 1902 (63); Berne, Klipstein, 'Zeichnungen 1650–1950', 1955 (1).

LIT. see *Catalogue* III and *Addenda*; also: E. W. Kornfeld, in *Du*, XIX, Oct. 1959,
pp.43ff.

146

Sir Peter Paul Rubens (1577–1640)

146 *Female Nude*

Red and black chalk heightened with white. 27×41·5
Inv. no.62

The pose of this sleeping figure, one of many variations on the theme, was perhaps originally inspired by Titian's *Bacchanal of the Andrians* (Prado), seen by Rubens in Rome. The drawing is thought to date from *c*.1630.

PROV. P. H. Lankrink (Lugt 2090); J. van Haecken (Lugt 2516); J. Richardson, Jnr. (Lugt 2170); Sir Joshua Reynolds (Lugt 2364); Gerald M. Fitzgerald, sold Sotheby, 23f. May 1922 (41). Acquired London 1941.

LIT. See *Catalogue* I and *Addenda*; subsequently: M. Bernhard, *Rubens Handzeichnungen*, 1977, p.431.

147

Sir Peter Paul Rubens (1577–1640)

147 *Helena Fourment*

Black and red chalk heightened with white. Pen and ink in the headdress and in some details of the head. 61·2×55 COLOUR PLATE XXII
The figure cut round in silhouette and backed
Inv. no.64

The portrait probably dates from the time of Rubens' marriage in 1630 to Helena Fourment (1614–73). She appears to be dressed for church and is holding a prayerbook with a gloved hand. With her bare right hand she draws back the 'huke' or 'heuke', a fashionable all-enveloping garment which was suspended from a tasselled skull cap and reached to the ground, protecting the wearer from wind and rain. The sheet is exceptional among Rubens' drawings in its scale and its rich and elaborate technique. It is presumably not a preparatory study for a painting, but an independent work.

PROV. Prince Charles de Lorraine; Comte de Cuypers; Schamp d'Averschoot, Ghent, sold Ghent, 1840 (192); Robert Stayner Holford; Sir George Lindsay Holford, sold Christie's, 17f. March 1928 (3); art market, Amsterdam, 1932. Acquired London 1934.

EXH. Burlington Fine Arts Club, 'Holford Pictures', 1921–2 (28); R.A., 'Flemish and Belgian Art', 1927 (570); Amsterdam, E. S. Wissellingh & Co., 'Dutch and Flemish Pictures, 17th cent.', 1932 (14); British Museum, 'Rubens', 1977 (155).

LIT. See *Catalogue 1* and *Addenda*; subsequently: M. Bernhard, *Rubens Handzeichnungen*, 1977, p.444; exh. cat., *Die Rubenszeichnungen der Albertina*, Vienna, Albertina, 1977, p.124.

Sir Peter Paul Rubens (1577–1640)

148 *Study for the 'Bath of Diana'*

Pen and ink. 29·1×50·9
On the *verso* a study in red and black chalk for the Munich *Lion Hunt* of *c*.1622, and some indistinct writing in the artist's hand
Inv. no.65

The drawing on the *recto* is generally agreed to be later than the *verso* drawing. Datings have been proposed in the later 1620s, the early or, more convincingly, later 1630s. The studies are for Rubens' painting known as the *Bath of Diana* (Rotterdam, Museum Boymans van Beuningen), which is the surviving right half of a damaged *Diana and Actaeon*. Rubens was clearly inspired by Titian's painting of the subject (Sutherland coll., National Gallery of Scotland), which he would have seen in Spain.

PROV. P. H. Lankrink (Lugt 2090); J. Richardson, Jnr. (Lugt 2170); R. Adam Ellis, sold Sotheby, 18 Dec. 1940 (15). Acquired London 1941.

LIT. See *Addenda*; subsequently (LIT. for *verso* not included): F.-A. Dreier, in *Niederdeutsche Beiträge zur Kunstgeschichte*, XVI, p.47.

148

149

150

151

Giovanni Battista Tiepolo (1696–1770)

149 *Satyr and Satyress*

Pen and ink and wash over black chalk. 14·7×27·1
Laid down
Inscribed in a later hand, 'Tiepolo'
Inv. no.380

Hitherto connected with the satyrs in Tiepolo's ceiling painting at the Palazzo Clerici, Milan, and dated accordingly to *c*.1740. The sheet differs, however, from other drawings of satyrs associated with that ceiling. The appearance of the present pair and their suggested setting indicate, rather, that they could be experimental studies for the four pairs of satyrs which form part of the ceiling decoration of the Ballroom of the Villa Pisani at Strà, painted 1760–62.

PROV. Group-Capt. P. M. Dobree-Bell, sold Sotheby, 8 July 1964 (84). Acquired London 1966.

EXH. Alfred Brod Gall., 'Old Master Drawings', 1965 (32).

Giovanni Battista Tiepolo (1696–1770)

150 *Portrait of one of the Artist's Sons (?)*

Red chalk heightened with white on blue paper. 23·6×16·1
Inscribed on the *verso*, 'Xrs 12 No.3465' (price and serial no. possibly in Domenico Tiepolo's hand)
Inv. no.161

From the 'Wendland Sketchbook'. The identification of the sitter is traditional and cannot be confirmed. The drawing is thought to date from the years in Würzburg, *c*.1751–3. A copy is in the 'Würzburg Third Sketchbook', perhaps by Lorenzo Tiepolo. (For information in this entry and Numbers 183, 184, see Knox, 1980, under LIT.).

PROV. Domenico Tiepolo(?); J. D. Bossi (1767–1853); C. C. F. Beyerlen (1826–1881), sold Gutekunst, Stuttgart, 1882; Dr. H. Wendland, Lugano. Acquired Vienna 1936.

LIT. See *Addenda*; subsequently: G. Knox, *Giambattista and Domenico Tiepolo . . . The Chalk Drawings*, 1980, p.284 (M631).

Giovanni Battista Tiepolo (1696–1770)

151 *The Holy Family with S. Joseph Reading*

Pen and ink and wash. 28·5×21·5
Inv. no.159

There are a large number of pen drawings by Tiepolo of the Holy Family similar in type to the present one. Three are in this collection, all dated to the 1750s; Number 151, dated to *c*.1757, is exceptional in its fine condition.

PROV. Sale, Sotheby, 31 May 1932 (16); T. Harris, London; C. R. and A. P. Rudolf, sold Sotheby, 2 Nov. 1949 (39). Acquired at sale.

EXH. Burlington Fine Arts Club, 1936–7 (86); Matthiesen Gallery, 1939 (120).

152

153

Jacopo Tintoretto (1518–1594)

152 *Studies after Michelangelo's 'Samson and the Philistines'*

Charcoal on green-grey paper, heightened with white. 45·2×27·4
Laid down
Inv. no.99

One of a group of drawings by Tintoretto and his studio after Michelangelo's projected group of *Samson and the Philistines*. The artist may have seen Michelangelo's original model, now lost, and probably had a copy or cast of it. The number of such studies is greater perhaps than those by Tintoretto after Michelangelo's Medici Tomb figures (drawing in this collection, inv. no.100, not on exhibition). The present drawing, dating perhaps from the early 1550s, is probably an autograph rather than studio work.

PROV. Acquired Paris 1954.

LIT. P. Rossi, *I Disegni di Jacopo Tintoretto*, 1975, p.43.

Antoine Watteau (1684–1721)

153 *A Faun*

Black, red and white chalk. 28·5×21·1
Inv. no.221

Study for the faun in *L'Automne*, one of a series of *The Seasons* painted by Watteau for Pierre Crozat's dining room. The painting is lost, but is recorded in an engraving by Faissar. The date of *'Les Saisons Crozat'* is not known, but *c.*1716 has been proposed.

PROV. M. Auguste, sold Paris, 28ff. May 1850(?); Baron Schwiter (Lugt 1768), sold Drouot, Paris, 20f. April 1883; H. Michel Levy, sold Paris, 12f. May 1919 (pl.116); A. Fauchier-Magnan, sold Sotheby, 4 Dec. 1935 (66). Acquired at sale. (There is an unidentified collector's mark.)

LIT. See *Catalogue* III.

154

Fra Bartolommeo (1472–1517)

154 *A Tree in Winter*

Pen and ink. 28·7×21·2

Inv. no.84

For the history and dating see Number 124 in Selection A.

PROV. as for Number 124.

LIT. as for Number 124.

155

Pieter Bruegel the Elder(?) (*c*.1525/30–1569)

155 *Seated Burgher*

Pen and ink over black chalk. 18·9×15·2
Trimmed probably on all sides
Inscribed in the artist's hand with numerous colour notes, and, lower right, in a different but not much later hand, 'Pet Brugell'
On the *verso:* Burgher seated on a low wall and a cripple
Inv. no.7

One of a group of studies, to which Number 156 also belongs, known as 'naer het leven' ('from the life'). Traditionally these have been attributed to Pieter Bruegel the Elder, but their authorship has been much disputed over a number of years, and they are now accepted by many as the work of Roelandt Savery (1576(?)–1639). There still appears to be some ground for retaining the traditional attribution. A date in the 1550s has been suggested for the present drawing.

PROV. The Rt. Hon. Henry Hobhouse, until 1935; E. E. Huxtable. Acquired London 1943.

LIT. See *Catalogue* 1 and *Addenda*.

Pieter Bruegel the Elder(?) (*c*.1525/30–1569)

156 *A Mule in Harness*

Pen and ink over faint traces of black chalk. 9·5×15·6
Trimmed probably on all sides. Inscribed in the artist's hand with colour-notes and, lower right, 'naer het leŭen'
On the *verso:* A man seen from the back
Inv. no.318

One of the group of studies 'naer het leven', for which see under Number 155. *A Mule in Harness* is closely comparable with a drawing in Vienna, *Team of Horses*

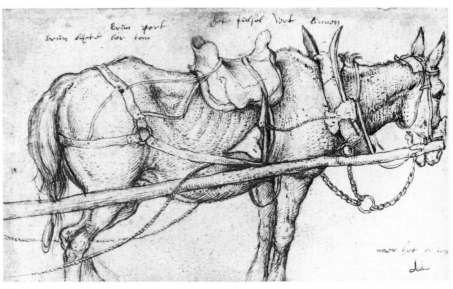

156

PLATE XIX Oskar Kokoschka *Market in Tunis* cat.34

PLATE XX Hugo van der Goes *A Saint, Seated, holding a Book on her Knees* cat.167

PLATE XXI Rembrandt van Rijn *The Artist's Wife, Saskia, Standing* cat.142

PLATE XXII Sir Peter Paul Rubens *Helena Fourment* cat.147

157

(Albertina), and may be dated, if indeed by Bruegel, to the later 1550s. The figure on the *verso* seems close to one in a painting by Roelandt Savery (*The Kermesse*, D. Flower coll.), but this could signify only that Savery was familiar with Bruegel's drawings.

PROV. Lionel Lucas (Lugt, *Suppl.*, 1733a); Claude Lucas, sold Christie's, 9 Dec. 1949 (64). Acquired London 1955.

LIT. See *Catalogue* IV.

Paul Cézanne (1839–1906)

157 *A Statue under Trees*

Pencil and watercolour. 48·2×31·3
Inv. no.240

This watercolour is thought to be a late work, of the second half of the 1890s.

PROV. Acquired 1941 from Sir Kenneth Clark.

LIT. See *Catalogue* III.

Claude Gellée, called Claude Lorrain (1600–1682)

158 *A Clump of Trees*

Black chalk and brown wash. 22×30·8
Inv. no.417

Signed and dated on the *verso*, 'Claude Gellee IV Roma 1650' (the '5' written over a '6'). Framed by the artist at left and faintly along the top in wash; this, and the surrounding blank margin, probably indicate that Claude himself considered this study a work of art in its own right.

158

159

PROV. Charles Morin (Lugt 597)?; New York art market, *c.*1960. Acquired London 1963.

EXH. Arts Council, Hayward Gallery, 'Claude Lorrain', 1969 (86).

LIT. See *Catalogue* VI.

Edgar Degas (1834–1917)

159 *Study of a Horse and Jockey*

Pencil. 20×16·5
Inv. no.237

Not identified among the drawings in the sales of Degas' *atelier* (see PROV.), although a number of similar ones were in the fourth sale (2f. July 1919). Degas' first paintings of the racecourse date from the 1860s; the present drawing may belong to the later 1860s or early 1870s. Mr. William Bradford has suggested that the drawing, which is on semi-transparent paper, may be a tracing; no source has yet been established.

PROV. Degas' *atelier* (Lugt 657); Gustave Pellet; Maurice Exsteens. Acquired New York 1955.

EXH. Kansas City, William Rockhill Nelson Gallery of Art, 1955.

Eugène Delacroix (1798–1863)

160 *Two Branches with Leaves*

Pencil and watercolour. 25·3×39·2
Dated, lower left, in the artist's handwriting, 'Champrosay 28 oct 60'
Inv. no.235

Delacroix had bought a house at Champrosay, near the forest of Sénart, in 1844.

PROV. Sale after his death of contents of artist's studio, Paris, 17ff. Feb. 1864 (Lugt 838). Acquired Paris 1953.

160

161

Albrecht Dürer (1471–1528)

161 *One of the Wise Virgins*

Pen and ink. 29·1×20·4
Inscribed, top centre, by a later hand, with the (wrong) date, 1508, and 'A.D.'
and, lower left, '9'
On the *verso*: Two studies of a man's left leg; dated, by the artist, 1493

162

Inv. no.251

An outstanding work from Dürer's *Wanderjahre* (1490–94). For part of 1493, the year of this drawing, Dürer was in Strasbourg. He had been to Colmar, hoping to meet Martin Schongauer, who had however just died (1491). The influence of Schongauer can be seen in this, as in other works of the artist at that time. It has been suggested that a lost project by Schongauer for a series of the Wise and Foolish Virgins might be the source of Dürer's drawing.

PROV. Sir Thomas Lawrence (Lugt 2445); Rietschel coll., sold Dresden, 1862 (621); Sir Charles Murray; C. W. Murray, sold Sotheby, 27 April 1927 (89); H. Oppenheimer, sold Christie's, 10ff. July 1936 (365). Acquired at sale.

EXH. Nuremberg, Germanisches Museum, 'Dürer', 1928 (240).

LIT. See *Catalogue* III and *Addenda;* subsequently: J. Rowlands in exh. cat., *The Graphic Work of Albrecht Dürer*, British Museum, 1971, under no.12.

Albrecht Dürer (1471–1528)

162 *Studies of Two Horsemen*

Brush and (?) pen, two shades of ink, wash. 13×12·1
Probably a fragment; scribbles in ink at top centre, and two wavy lines in grey ink, lower left
Laid down
Inv. no.252

The technique of drawing with the tip of the brush is unusual for Dürer, and this once led to some doubt of the authenticity of this sheet. It can however be accepted, probably without reserve, as an autograph work of *c*.1493–4. The horsemen on this fragmentary sheet may belong to a larger composition, perhaps of a *Crucifixion*. A drawing in the British Museum, *The Virgin with S. John and the Weeping Women,* is in a similar technique, and may be connected with the same Calvary scene.

PROV. Antonio Tempesta (? monogram showing through from *verso*); John Skippe (1742–1812; Lugt 2798 and *Suppl.*); by descent to E. H. Martin, sold Christie's, 20f. Nov. 1958 (299). Acquired at sale.

EXH. R.A. (Diploma Gallery), 'Drawings by Old Masters', 1953 (219).

LIT. See *Catalogue* III; subsequently: J. Rowlands in exh. cat., *The Graphic Work of Albrecht Dürer*, British Museum, 1971, under no.13.

Albrecht Dürer (1471–1528)

163 *The Emperors Charlemagne and Sigismund*

Pen and watercolour. 17·7×20·6
Folded down centre to indicate wings of diptych
Inv. no.253

On the left: Charlemagne's heraldic devices, the two-headed eagle and fleurs-de-lys; on the right: the Imperial two-headed eagle above Sigismund, flanked by blank shields inscribed by the artist with names of countries and corrected by a probably later hand.

This watercolour, in immaculate condition, is a preparatory study for the two large paintings of the emperors (*c*.2m. high, Nuremberg, Germanisches Museum), commissioned from Dürer by the town of Nuremberg in 1510. The

163

paintings were completed three years later, with numerous differences from the watercolour, and no longer forming a diptych, as projected here. They were intended for the 'Heiltumskammer', where the Imperial Insignia of the Holy Roman Empire were kept the night before an annual ceremony of display to the people.

PROV. Prince Heinrich Lubomirski; Lubomirski coll., Ossolinski Institute, Lvov (Lemberg), no.8298. Acquired 1954 from Prince Lubomirski.

EXH. Nuremberg, Germanisches Museum, 'Dürer', 1928 (373).

LIT. See *Catalogue* III and *Addenda*; subsequently: Earl E. Rosenthal, in *Jahrbuch der Kunsthistorischen Sammlung in Wien*, N. F. xxx, 1970, pp.33ff; F. Anzelewsky, *Albrecht Dürer. Das Malerische Werk*, 1971, pp.48, 81, 97, 233.

Sir Anthony van Dyck (1599–1641)

164 *S. Mary Magdalene*

Black chalk heightened with white on blue-grey paper. 27·9×22
Laid down
Inv. no.328

S. Mary Magdalene appears a number of times in this pose, usually in reverse, in van Dyck's *Crucifixions*. The drawing may be preparatory to a finished painting, or a *ricordo* used more than once. Its style indicates van Dyck's second period in Antwerp, *c*.1628–32.

PROV. Acquired London 1963.

164

165

Noemi Ferenczy (1890–1947)

165 *Design for a Tapestry*

Gouache on transparent paper. 37·4×40·2
Inv. no.277

Datable to the winter of 1936–7. A closely similar version exists, but with different colours, entitled *Meadow in Flower* (present whereabouts unknown). A tapestry by the same Hungarian artist, *A Girl lying in a Meadow*, 1932, was formerly with the present collection; a number of drawings by her brother, Benjamin (Béni) Ferenczy, are still in the collection.

PROV. Acquired 1937 from the artist.

EXH. Budapest, Galerie Frankel, 1937 (20).

Jean Honoré Fragonard (1732–1806)

166 *The Shaded Walk ('L'Allée ombreuse')*

Watercolour over pencil. 16·6×14·9
Laid down
Inv. no.230

The frontal view of a path receding sharply beneath a tunnel of trees was a subject which especially attracted Fragonard, and also later French artists, including Cézanne – compare, for instance, his Number 157 in this exhibition. The present drawing may be related to the painting, *A Shady Avenue* (New York, Metropolitan Museum), and has been dated to *c*.1775–80.

PROV. E. Rodrigues (Lugt 897); Jacques Guérin, sold 2of. Dec. 1922 (56, as H. Robert); Albert Henraux; Tony Mayer, Paris, sold Charpentier, Paris, 3 Dec. 1957 (3). Acquired at sale.

LIT. See *Addenda*.

167

Hugo van der Goes (*c*.1440–1482)

167 *A Saint, Seated, holding a Book on her Knees*

Brush and grey ink and white body-colour on green prepared ground
23×18·9   COLOUR PLATE XX
Laid down. Trimmed probably on all sides
Inscribed on *recto* (lower right, cut), '787' (?), and on the backing, in 16th-cent.(?) hand, 'Pietro Perugino' and 'sandro scrive che sicurro sia'
Inv. no.314

This is generally accepted as one of the artist's rare surviving drawings, comparable with the *Jacob and Rachel* at Oxford (Christ Church), and datable to the same period as *The Portinari Altarpiece* (Uffizi), *c*.1475. A special feature of the drawing is that certain details indicate that it is a *'ricordo'*, copied by the artist from his own altarpiece, now lost, but known in what must be a close copy, *The Madonna enthroned with Saints* by The Master of 1499 (Richmond, Virginia). Furthermore, the frequent repetition of this figure in subsequent Flemish painting and manuscript illumination had led, even before this drawing was known, to the supposition that there was a common prototype in a celebrated painting.

PROV. Presumably 16th-cent. Italian coll. (see inscriptions on *verso*); private coll., France; M. L. Rosenthal, Berne, 1935; L. V. Randall, Montreal, sold Sotheby, 10 May 1961 (4). Acquired at sale.

166

168

EXH. Paris, Orangerie, 'De Van Eyck à Bruegel', 1935 (196); Cambridge (Mass.), Fogg Museum, '70 Master Drawings', 1948–9 (7); Victoria and Albert Museum, 'Drawing: Technique and Purpose', 1981 (197).

LIT. See *Catalogue* IV and *Addenda*; subsequently: J. Byam Shaw, *Drawings by Old Masters at Christ Church, Oxford*, 1976, p.320 under no.1309.

Oskar Kokoschka (1886–1980)

168 *Various Flowers*

Watercolour. 62×45·9
Signed, lower right, 'O. Kokoschka
Inv. no.270

One of a group of three flower pieces by the artist in this collection, all dating from 1939/40

PROV. Acquired from the artist, 1939/40.

169

Leonardo da Vinci (1452–1519)

169 *Studies for a S. Mary Magdalene*

Pen and ink. 13·7×17·9
Inv. no.80

All the artist's framing lines are visible, but it is probably a fragment of a larger sheet. The subject of these studies cannot be connected with any known work by Leonardo, although the pose of the upper figure suggests comparison with the portrait of *Cecilia Gallerani* (Cracow). The drawing has been dated to *c.*1480, during Leonardo's first Florentine period.

PROV. Sir Thomas Lawrence (Lugt 2445); Samuel Woodburn, sold Christie's, 4ff. June 1860, no.1051 (1); Sir Thomas Phillipps; by descent, T. Fitzroy Phillipps Fenwick. Acquired with the Fenwick coll., 1946.

EXH. R.A. (Diploma Gallery), 'Leonardo Quincentenary', 1952 (4).

LIT. See *Catalogue* II.

Andrea Mantegna (1431–1506)

170 *Studies for Christ at the Column*

Pen and ink. 23·4×14·4
Inv. no.345

On the *verso* are further studies for Christ at the column, not visible until 1958 when the old backing was removed from the drawing. The figures on both *recto* and *verso* are connected with a *Flagellation of Christ* by Mantegna, known through two 15th-century engravings, for which the model may have been a painting, now lost. It was the publication of the *recto* of this drawing in 1930 which aroused the general and continuing controversy over the attribution of drawings to Mantegna or Bellini. Acquired as a Bellini, the present drawing is now securely assigned to Mantegna and dated to *c.*1460.

PROV. John Skippe (1742–1812; Lugt 2798 and *Suppl.*); by descent to E. H. Martin, sold Christie's, 20f. Nov. 1958 (36, as Giovanni Bellini). Acquired at sale.

EXH. R.A., 'Italian Art', 1930 (708); Birmingham, 'Art Treasures of the Midlands', 1934 (210); R.A. (Diploma Gallery) 'Drawings by Old Masters', 1953 (17).

LIT. See *Catalogue* V and *Addenda*.

Michelangelo (1475–1564)

171 *Christ before Pilate*

Pen and ink over some red chalk. 21×28·2
Inv. no.422 (not in *Catalogue*)

On the *verso* are parts of two unfinished sonnets by Michelangelo, studies of a leg, a torso and a head in red chalk and a pen-and-ink sketch of a slave, perhaps for the tomb of Julius II. At the top of the *recto* is also a study for a leg. Although part, at least, of the *verso* of this sheet has always been accepted as by Michelangelo there has in the past been some disagreement about the authorship of the *recto*. To many, these doubts seem now to be resolved, although the subject cannot with

171

certainty be related to any known or recorded work. It has been proposed (by J. Wilde, unpublished) that it may be connected with the commission for the unexecuted façade of S. Lorenzo in Florence in 1516, a date which is supported by the style of the drawing. The design indicates a project for relief-sculpture, the hatching suggesting chisel marks. The scene may represent S. Lawrence brought before the prefect, rather than Christ before Pilate (See Tolnay, 1975, under LIT.). (Unpublished notes by J. Wilde used for this entry.)

PROV. P. J. Mariette (Lugt 1852); by 1928, Sir Robert Witt (Lugt, *Suppl.*, 2228b) until 1943; Dr. and Mrs. Francis Springell, sold Sotheby, 28 June 1962(17). Acquired 1963 from Dr. Bodmer, Geneva.

EXH. Victoria and Albert Museum, 'Old Masters from the Witt Coll.', 1943, p.25; British Museum, 'Michelangelo', 1953 (40); R.A. (Diploma Gallery), 'Drawings by Old Masters', 1953 (40); Colnaghi, 'Old Master Drawings from the Springell Coll.', 1959 (24); British Museum, 'Michelangelo', 1975 (77).

LIT. K. Tolnai in *Münchner Jahrbuch*, N.F. V, 1928, pp.70ff.; A. Venturi in *L'Arte*, XXXI, 1928, pp.155f.; B. Berenson, *The Drawings of the Florentine Painters*, 2nd ed., 1938, nos. 1696A (*recto*), 1543A (*verso*); C. de Tolnay, *Michelangelo*, III, 1948, no.104; L. Dussler, *Die Zeichnungen des Michelangelo*, 1959, no.216; F. Hartt, *Michelangelo Drawings*, 1971, nos.131 (*recto*), 130 (*verso*); C. de Tolnay, *Corpus dei Disegni di Michelangelo*, I, 1975, no.101.

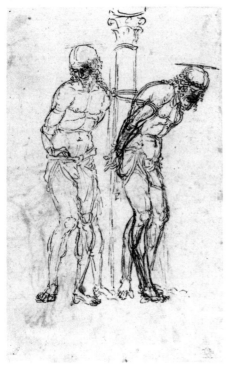

170

Michelangelo (1475–1564)

172 *Christ on the Cross*

Black chalk. 27·5×23·4
Inscribed with the artist's name, lower left, in late 18th or early 19th-cent. hand
Inv. no.426 (not in *Catalogue*)

One of a series of related drawings of Christ on the Cross, dating from Michelangelo's last years and all of an almost mystical intensity; in the others the Cross is flanked by the Virgin and S. John. The drawings are characterized technically by frequent alterations and repetitions of outline. Their purpose is not known. It has been proposed that they were for presentation to friends, or were studies for a projected but never executed sculptural group of the Crucifixion.

PROV. Acquired London 1940.

EXH. British Museum, 'Michelangelo', 1953 (104); British Museum, 'Michelangelo', 1975 (179).

LIT. R. Wittkower in *Burlington Magazine*, LXXVIII, 1941, pp.159f.; J. Wilde, *Italian Drawings . . .in the British Museum. Michelangelo and his Studio*, 1953, p.120; L. Dussler, *Die Zeichnungen des Michelangelo*, 1959, no.185; C. de Tolnay, *Michelangelo*, v, 1960, no.257; F. Hartt, *Michelangelo Drawings*, 1971, no.430; R. Haussherr, *Michelangelos Kruzifixus für Vittoria Colonna*, 1971, p.51; C. de Tolnay, *Corpus dei Disegni di Michelangelo*, III, 1978, no.420.

Girolamo Francesco Maria Mazzola, called Parmigianino (1503–1540)

173 *S. Mary Magdalene* (?)

Black chalk heightened with white. 23·1×17·5
Inscribed in ink by a later hand, on *recto* and *verso*, 'Permegiano' and in faded red ink, lower right, with numerals (?)
On the *verso*: the Virgin(?) spinning
Inv. no.96

The identification of the figures on the *recto* as S. Mary Magdalene and on the *verso* as the Virgin was challenged by Popham (1971, see LIT.), who considered both to be studies from the life. The *recto* was formerly thought to be made specifically in preparation for the etching known as *S. Thaïs*, which dates from the second half of the 1520s, the date also assigned then to Number 173. Popham considered the two not so directly connected, and suggested that Parmigianino may have made the present drawing, together with other related sheets, at Fontanellato, *c.*1524.

PROV. Dr. C. D. Ginsburg (Lugt 1145), sold Sotheby, 20ff. July 1915 (26?); H. S. Reitlinger, sold Sotheby, 9 Dec. 1953 (73). Acquired at sale.

LIT. See *Catalogue* II; subsequently: A. E. Popham, *Catalogue of the Drawings of Parmigianino*, 1971, no.764, and under no.60.

173

172 michelange.

174

Girolamo Francesco Maria Mazzola, called Parmigianino (1503–1540)

174 *The Conversion of S. Paul*

Pen and ink and wash heightened with white body-colour; faint traces of black chalk. 23·6×33
Faint inscriptions in red chalk on *verso*
On the *verso* is another version of the same subject, but showing the moment just after the conversion and the blinding rather than just before as is shown here.
Inv. no.360

Dated formerly to Parmigianino's Roman period, this sheet was considered by Popham (1971, see LIT.) to be a work of *c.*1527–30, contemporary with the painting of the subject in Vienna, for which there is a chalk study in this collection (inv. no.363, not on exhibition). The design of Number 174 has little in common with the painting except the figure of the fallen saint.

PROV. J. M. in a circle (Lugt, *Suppl.,* 1493a on *verso*). Acquired 1962 from Hugh Squire.

LIT. A. E. Popham, *Catalogue of the Drawings of Parmigianino,* 1971, no.768 (*recto* and *verso* reversed).

Pablo Picasso (1881–1973)

175 *Pigs*

Charcoal. 21·3×27·3
Signed, 'Picasso'. The signature was added in 1954, the year of exhibition
Inv. no.264

A study for a more elaborate drawing, *The Swineherd* (present location unknown),

175

made at Gosol in the Pyrenees, where Picasso spent the summer of 1906. Both drawings belonged to Gertrude Stein, who wrote (see LIT.), 'She [Gertrude Stein] was always fond of pigs, and because of this Picasso made and gave her some charming drawings of the prodigal son among the pigs. And one delightful study of pigs all by themselves.'

PROV. Gertrude Stein. Acquired Paris 1954.

EXH. Paris, Berggruen & Cie., 1954 (29).

LIT. see *Catalogue* III; also: Gertrude Stein, *The Autobiography of Alice B. Toklas*, 1933, p.100.

Bernardino Pinturicchio(?) (*c*.1454–1513)

176 *Study of a flying Angel*

Metalpoint, pen (and brush) and ink, heightened with white body-colour, on prepared grey ground. 21·7×13·9
On the *verso,* a standing man seen from the back
Inv. no.81

176

The drawings on both *recto* and *verso* record figures in Perugino's Sistine Chapel frescoes (completed 1482), and both recur in the work of his assistant, Pinturicchio. It appears likely that the drawings on both sides of this sheet are not preparatory but records copied from Perugino by Pinturicchio and used in his workshop. The *Flying Angel,* which derives from the fresco destroyed to make way for Michelangelo's *Last Judgement,* appears in Pinturicchio's *Glory of S. Bernardino* in S. Maria d'Aracoeli in Rome (1484). The drawing on the *verso* is possibly not by the same hand. The sheet has also been attributed to Giovanni Santi.

PROV. Sir Thomas Lawrence (2445 on *verso*); W. Mayor (Lugt 2799); J. P. Heseltine (Lugt 1507 on *verso*); H. Oppenheimer, sold Christie's, 10ff. July 1936 (169, as by Giovanni Santi). Acquired London 1953.

LIT. see *Catalogue* II and *Addenda.*

177

Rembrandt van Rijn (1606–1669)

177 *Study of a seated Actor*

Pen and ink and wash. 18·5×14·4
On the *verso* a study of a head in pen ank ink, probably of the same model
Inv. no.406

There are a number of comparable studies of actors by Rembrandt. The present one is distinguished among them by its fine quality and by a bravado not commonly shown by Rembrandt's figures. It is considered to date from the mid-1630s.

PROV. E. Bouverie (Lugt 325); Lessing J. Rosenwald, Jenkintown (Penn.); Mrs. D. Monet Rosenwald, New York, sold Sotheby, 6 July 1967 (8). Acquired at sale.

178

EXH. Cambridge (Mass.), Pierpont Morgan Library and Fogg Museum, 'Rembrandt Drawings from American Colls.', 1960 (11).

LIT. see *Catalogue* VI.

Rembrandt van Rijn (1606–1669)

178 *A Recumbent Lion*

Pen and ink, washed; overlying colours in oil. 13·7×25·4
Laid down; on the backing an unidentified collector's mark
Inv. no.410

There are a number of studies by Rembrandt of resting lions, but none in oil or with the high degree of finish seen here. This particular combination of media is indeed very rare, if not unique, in the artist's work. A date of *c.*1650 has been proposed for the majority of the lion studies. Engraved by B. Picart in *Recueil de Lions*, 1729 (C.3).

PROV. Francis, 3rd Duke of Bridgewater; George Granville, 1st Duke of Sutherland; Lord Francis Egerton, 1st Earl of Ellesmere; by descent. Sold Christie's, 26 June 1964 (75). Acquired at sale.

Pierre-Auguste Renoir (1841–1919)

179 *Laundresses*

Pencil and pen and ink. 31·4×22·5
Laid down
Inv. no.243

A subject which Renoir drew and painted a number of times in the later 1880s, the probable date of the present drawing. Similar poses reappear in other works, including the painting of *Washerwomen* (Baltimore, Cone coll.).

PROV. Curt Glaser, sold Max Perl, Berlin, 18f. May 1933 (1261a). Acquired at sale.

LIT. see *Catalogue* III.

179

180

Sir Peter Paul Rubens (1577–1640)

180 *The Conversion of S. Paul*

Pen and ink and wash, white body-colour. 22·2×32·9
Laid down
Inv. no.57

This drawing, made probably on opposite pages of a sketchbook, has been separated in two parts throughout its known history until 1953. Except for recent literature (below) the two halves are therefore described here independently.

Left half: 22·2×16·5

On the *verso*, in pencil, 'Conversion of St. Paul, Vandyck, Lawrence coll^n' (?in Samuel Woodburn's hand).

PROV. P. H. Lankrink (Lugt 2090); Sir Joshua Reynolds (Lugt 2364); Sir Thomas Lawrence (Lugt 2445); 1940, Ashmolean Museum, Oxford (202). Acquired 1953 from the Ashmolean.

EXH. Wildenstein, 'Rubens', 1950 (42).

LIT. See *Catalogue* I.

PLATE XXIII Giovanni Battista Tiepolo *A King Kneeling* cat.183

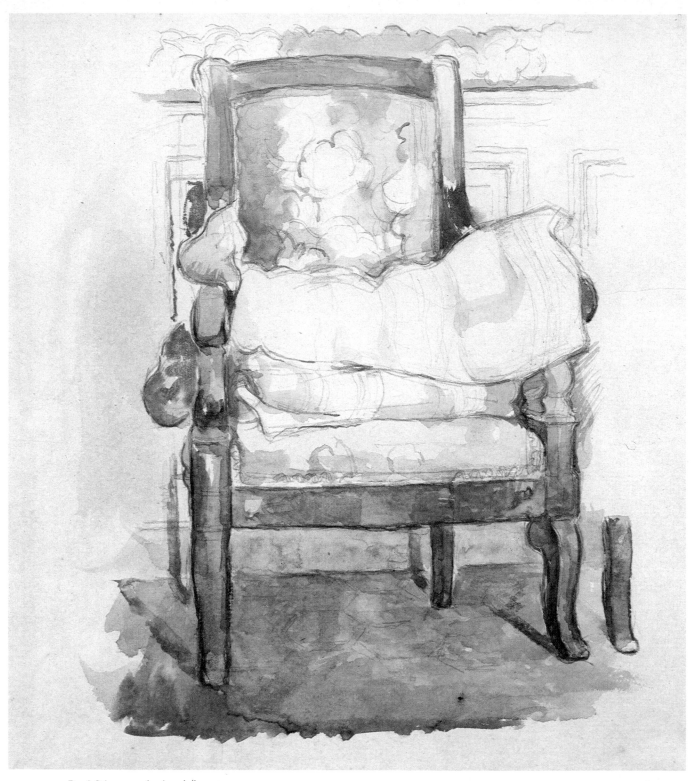

PLATE XXIV Paul Cézanne *An Armchaïr* cat.132

181

Right half: 22·2×16·4

On the *verso*, in Reynolds' hand, 'The picture is at Düsseldorf'.

PROV. P. H. Lankrink (Lugt 2090); Sir Joshua Reynolds (Lugt 2364); Sale, Boerner, Leipzig, 30f. March 1943 (124), bought Dr. Grote. Acquired Düsseldorf 1952.

LIT. See *Catalogue* I.

For further discussion see under painting Number 69.
For LIT. see also *Addenda*; subsequently: M. Waddingham in *Burlington Magazine*, CXIV, 1972, p.601; K. Renger in exh. cat., *Rubens in der Grafik*, Göttingen/ Hanover/Nuremberg, 1977, p.84; J. S. Held, *The Oil Sketches of Peter Paul Rubens*, 1980, p.462 and under no.421.

Sir Peter Paul Rubens (1577–1640)

181 *Study of a Wild Cherry Tree with Brambles and Weeds*

Black, red and white chalk and yellow pigment on light brown paper. 54·5×49·5
Laid down
Annotated in Flemish, by the artist, with the species and colours of the plants
Inv. no.63

Few plant studies by Rubens survive, and these are hard to date or to relate to paintings. The present study was formerly thought to be connected with *The Château de Steen* (*c.*1636; National Gallery), a theory apparently now rejected. The style of the drawing, however, suggests a date in the 1630s.

PROV. J. Richardson, Snr. (Lugt 2184); J. van Rijmsdijk (Lugt 2167); Sir Thomas Lawrence (Lugt 2445); Samuel Woodburn, sold Christie's, 4ff. June 1860, no.307 (2); Sir Thomas Phillipps; by descent, T. Phillipps Fenwick. Acquired with the Fenwick coll., 1946.

EXH. R.A., '17th-cent. Art', 1938 (580); British Museum, 'Rubens', 1977 (198).

LIT. See *Catalogue* I and *Addenda*; also: G. Martin, *National Gallery Catalogues. The Flemish School, c.1600–c.1900*, 1970, pp.140f.

Giovanni Battista Tiepolo (1696–1770)

182 *Apollo as Protector of the Arts*

Pen and ink and wash over traces of black chalk. 26·3×20·8
Inv. no.153

The drawing has been associated in style with a number of drawings in the Cheney Albums (Florence, Horne Foundation), and dated to *c.*1740.

PROV. W. Bateson; A. Fauchier-Magnan, sold Sotheby, 4 Dec. 1935 (53). Acquired at sale.

EXH. Burlington Fine Arts Club, 'Venetian 18th cent.', 1911 (63).

LIT. See *Catalogue* II.

Giovanni Battista Tiepolo (1696–1770)

183 *A King Kneeling*

Red chalk heightened with white on blue-grey paper   COLOUR PLATE XXIII
31·2×22·5
Inscribed on the *verso*, 'No.3393', and other signs (possibly in Domenico Tiepolo's hand)
Inv. no.167

At one time considered to be a *ricordo* drawing by Domenico Tiepolo copied from the central figure in Giovanni Battista's *Adoration of the Kings* (Munich, Alte Pinakothek). This and a large number of similar sheets have recently been analysed by G. Knox (see LIT., 1980) and shown convincingly to be working drawings produced by Giovanni Battista himself. The date of the present sheet must therefore be *c.*1753, when the artist was working on the altarpiece.

PROV. Domenico Tiepolo(?); J. D. Bossi (1767–1853); C. C. F. Beyerlen (1826–1881), sold Gutekunst, Stuttgart, 1882; Sale, Gilhofer and Ranschburg, Lucerne, 28 June 1934 (294). Acquired at sale.

LIT. See *Catalogue* II and *Addenda*; subsequently: G. Knox, *Giambattista and Domenico Tiepolo . . . The Chalk Drawings*, 1980, pp.48, 246 (M293).

183

182

Giovanni Battista Tiepolo (1696–1770)

184 *An Angel holding a Monstrance*

Red and white chalk on blue-grey paper. 31·4×25·1
Inscribed on the *verso*, 'f(?) 48 Xrs No.3190' (price and serial no. possibly in Domenico Tiepolo's hand)
Inv. no.168

A drawing of the same category as Number 183. Its attribution to G. B. Tiepolo was doubted because it was thought to be a *ricordo* drawing. The evidence given by G. Knox (see LIT., 1980) appears to establish its position as a working drawing by Giovanni Battista for the last stage of his altarpiece for Aranjuez, *S. Paschal Baylon*, *c.*1769–70. For further discussion see under painting Number 111.

PROV. Domenico Tiepolo(?); J. D. Bossi (1767–1853); C. C. F. Beyerlen (1826–1881), sold Gutekunst, Stuttgart, 1882; H. Oppenheimer, sold Christie's, 10ff. July 1936 (180). Acquired London 1938.

LIT. See *Catalogue* II and *Addenda*; also: M. Levey in *Burlington Magazine*, CII, 1960, p.123; subsequently: G. Knox, *Giambattista and Domenico Tiepolo . . . The Chalk Drawings*, 1980, p.246 (M294).

184

Appendix I

Paintings in the Princes Gate Collection not on exhibition

Oskar Kokoschka (1886–1980)

Triptych: The Myth of Prometheus

Tempera on canvas
(a) Hades and Persephone 230×230
(b) Apocalypse 230×350
(c) Prometheus 230×230
Inv. no.260

These three canvases of 1950 were, at the time of execution, Kokoschka's largest; they were succeeded in 1954 by a comparable triptych, *Thermopylae* (Hamburg). The present triptych was conceived as a ceiling decoration for this collection, the first idea suggested late in 1949 (drawing for *Apocalypse*, formerly in this collection), and contracts dated 14 Jan. (*Apocalypse*) and 9 Mar. 1950 (*Hades and Persephone* and *Prometheus*); the whole completed in summer 1950. The group of symbols, lower left, in *Prometheus* was an added afterthought to the picture and *Hades and Persephone* was considerably altered at an advanced stage. The latter canvas is a substitution for a painting of *Amor and Psyche*, begun but rejected for this series, finished at Villeneuve in 1955, and now in a private collection; a lithograph and tapestry are based on it. In Kokoschka's explanation of the triptych (in various publications, see LIT. below) he claimed a deliberate disregard for current fashions and a return to the mainstream of European artistic tradition and Baroque principles of space and movement. Prometheus himself (260c) was seen — unusually — as a symbol of man's intellectual arrogance, doomed by the Fates to the 'realm of the mothers' (260a), where Persephone springs from the arms of Hades (a self-portrait) with a promise of regeneration. In the centrepiece (260b) Christian imagery and classical mythology are combined; on the hill to the left various scenes and figures represent the forces in the world of good and evil; to the right are approaching shades from the underworld and the four horses of the Apocalypse.

PROV. Commissioned and executed for this collection 1950.

EXH. Venice, Biennale XXVI, 1952, room XLVI (2); Arts Council, Tate Gallery, 'Kokoshka', 1962 (137).

LIT. See *Catalogue* III and *Addenda*; also: J. P. Hodin in *Bekenntnis zu Kokoschka*, 1963, pp.163ff.

Bernardino Licinio (before 1491–after 1549)

Portrait of a Lady

Canvas. 101·5×79
Inv. no.334

Formerly attributed variously to Paris Bordone, Titian and Moretto. This damaged portrait of a middle-aged lady had been overpainted to give the appearance of a young and handsome woman, as discovered when the picture was cleaned in 1961. The evident influence of Titian's *La Bella* (1536; Florence, Pitti) indicates a fairly late date in Licinio's career.

PROV. Baron Lazzaroni (or Lanfranconi), Paris; Marcell von Nemes, Munich; Baron Herzog, Budapest. Acquired Vienna 1961.

EXH. Budapest, 1937–8 (9), as by Paris Bordone.

LIT. See *Catalogue* V.

Lorenzo Lotto (*c.*1480–1556)

Portrait of a Man with a Skull

Canvas. 113×88·5
Inv. no.74
Old inventory number, '49', lower right.

Surface and paint-texture severely damaged. The portrait recalls the *Old Man with Gloves* (Brera, Milan), in composition and in the pose of the sitter, suggesting a date in the mid-1540s.

PROV. Sale, American Art Galleries, New York, Dec. 1924 (123); Paolo Paolini, Rome. Acquired Vienna 1928.

LIT. See *Catalogue* II; also: *Catalogue* 1937, no.20; subsequently: R. Pallucchini and G. Mariani Canova, *L'Opera completa del Lotto*, 1975, p.119 (246); F. Caroli, *Lorenzo Lotto e la nascita della psicologia moderna*, 1980, p.282.

Spanish School, Early Sixteenth Century

The Lamentation (front); *SS. Clara and Elizabeth of Thuringia* (back)

Panel. 83×81
Inv. no.255

In the *Lamentation* the haloes bear the names 'Sant Ian', 'Santa Maria', and 'Santa Maria Madalen'.

This panel, of unusual format, has been dated to the first decade of the 16th century.

PROV. Acquired 1930 from the Tolnay coll.

LIT. *Catalogue* 1937, no.2; forthcoming publication: E. Young in *Burlington Magazine*, 1981.

Appendix II

The following paintings catalogued by Count Seilern are no longer in the collection:

Inv. no.45   Sir Anthony van Dyck, *Madonna and Child with S. Dorothy (after Titian)*

Inv. no.106   Domenico Fetti, *The Return of the Prodigal Son*

Inv. no.202   Émile Vernet, *A Monk painting at an Easel*

Inv. no.212   Édouard Detaille, *A Hussar on Horseback*

Inv. no.213   Jean François Raffaëlli, *Young Girl Holding a Mirror*

Appendix III

Drawings in the Princes Gate Collection not exhibited in selections A and B

The titles of some of the drawings are abbreviated. The numerals refer to the inv. no.

Fra Bartolommeo

A Northern Village (recto); *A Town on the Banks of a River* (verso), 85

A Path leading between overhanging Rocks (recto); *Three Houses in a Village* (verso), 86

A Steep Rise of Rocky Ground (recto); *Buildings and a Hayrick* (verso), 89

A Windswept Bank, 87

Study for S. Mary Magdalene (recto *and* verso), 348

Study for 'Job', 350

Study for 'S. Mark', 349

The Approach to a Mountain Village, 83

Jacopo Bassano

A Gondolier, 98

Stefano Della Bella

An Army advancing, 122

Feluccas in Harbour, 121

Six Drawings on one Mount, 120

Three Drawings on one Mount, 117

Three Drawings on one Mount, 118

Three Drawings on one Mount, 119

Three Drawings on one Mount, 123

Two Drawings on one Mount, 116

Giuseppe Bernardino Bison

A Group of Figures with Bacchus, 147

Landscape with a leaning Tree, 390

The Flight into Egypt, 148

Hieronymus Bosch

S. Christopher, 178

Andrea Boscoli

Head of a Young Girl, 104

Serafino Brizzi

Designs for Stage Scenery, 126

Pieter Bruegel the Elder

Alpine Landscape, 10

An Alpine Landscape, 315

A Peasant carrying a Jar (recto); *A Man seen from the Back* (verso), 319

Landscape with a Town, 316

Landscape with two Mules, 8

Rocky Landscape with a Castle, 12

Pieter Bruegel the Elder (?)

Landscape with a Castle on a Rock, 320

Claude Gellée, called Claude Lorrain

An Ox (recto *and* verso), 414

Landscape with Trees and Buildings (recto); *Studies of a Bull* (verso), 214

Pastoral Scene in a Clearing (recto); *Study of a Tree* (verso), 416

Two Cows and a Calf, 415

Claude Gellée, called Claude Lorrain, attrib.

Study of a Tree, 216

Lovis Corinth

Centaurs embracing, 263

Antonio Allegri, called Correggio

Christ in 'The Coronation of the Virgin', 352

Putto blowing a Pipe(?), 353

Giambattista Crosato

S. Charles Borromeo, 127

Eugène Delacroix

A Moroccan Jewess, 419

Copy of the Child from Rubens' 'La Vierge au Perroquet', 420

Sheet with two Studies of a Female Nude, etc., 234

Sir Anthony van Dyck

A Sheet of Studies after Giulio Romano, 393

Christ on the Cross with S. Mary Magdalene (recto); *Landscape* (verso), 329

Sir Anthony van Dyck(?)

Study of a Man and of a Woman attacking another Woman, 68

The Martyrdom of S. Lawrence, 327

Adam Elsheimer(?)

Landscape with a Wayfarer, 254

Benjamin Ferenczy

'Eqilibre [sic] Evropeen', 283

Female Head, 278

Free Copies after Rubens, 281

Portrait of the Artist's Wife, 280

Studies of a Nude Boy, 279

Two Sketches of an Equestrian Statuette, 284, 285

Concordance for the Paintings

Inv. no.	cat. no.	Inv. no.	cat. no.	Inv. no.	cat. no.	Inv. no.	cat. no.
1	45	47	28	211	56	338	39
2	7	48	91	212	Appendix II	339	52
3	44	49	92	213	Appendix II	340	105
4	2	69	14	249	1	341	107
5	8	70	4	250	33	342	112
6	9	71	123	255	Appendix I	343	116
13	58	72	48	257	34	346	41
14	59	73	37	258	35	391	103
15	61	74	Appendix I	259	36	392	104
16	64	75	6	260	Appendix I	394	38
17	65	76	117	261	122	395	109
18	66	77	118	262	29	396	110
19	67	78	120	295	43	413	11
20	68	105	31	296	3		
21	69	106	Appendix II	297	27		
22	70	107	25	298	60		
23	71	108	26	299	62		
24	80	109	57	300	63		
25	73	110	13	301	72		
26	74	111	53	302	22		
27	75	112	47	303	24		
28	76	113	30	304	93		
29	77	170	106	305	94		
30	78	171	108	306	95		
31	81	172	111	307	96		
32	82	173	113	308	97		
33	79	174	114	309	98		
34	12	175	115	310	99		
35	83	176	90	311	100		
36	84	177	32	312	101		
37	85	201	5	313	102		
38	86	202	Appendix II	330	42		
39	87	203	18	331	121		
40	88	204	15	332	54		
41	89	205	51	333	55		
42	19	206	40	334	Appendix I		
43	20	207	16	335	49		
44	21	208	17	336	50		
45	Appendix II	209	10	337	119		
46	23	210	46				

Index of Artists

The numerals refer to the catalogue number of the exhibits